ENGRAVINGS.

NERO

CHAPTER I.
NERO'S MOTHER.

IN ancient times, when the city of Rome
was at the height of its power and splendor, it was the custom, as it is in fact now
with the inhabitants of wealthy capitals, for
the principal families to possess, in addition
to their city residences, rural villas for summer retreats, which they built in picturesque
situations, at a little distance from the city,
sometimes in the interior of the country, and
sometimes upon the sea-shore. There were
many attractive places of resort of this nature
in the neighborhood of Rome. Among them
was Antium.

Antium was situated on the sea-coast about
thirty miles south of the Tiber. A bold promontory here projects into the sea, affording

from its declivities the most extended and
magnificent views on every side. On the
north, looking from the promontory of Antium,
the eye follows the line of the coast away to
the mouth of the Tiber; while, on the south,
the view is terminated, at about the same distance, by the promontory of Circe, which is
the second cape, or promontory, that marks
the shore of Italy in going southward from
Rome. Toward the interior, from Antium,
there extends a broad and beautiful plain,
bounded by wooded hills toward the shore,
and by ranges of mountains in the distance
beyond. On the southern side of the cape,
and sheltered by it, was a small harbor where
vessels from all the neighboring seas had been
accustomed to bring in their cargoes, or to
seek shelter in storms, from time immemorial.
In fact, Antium, in point of antiquity, takes
precedence, probably, even of Rome.

The beauty and the salubrity of Antium
made it a very attractive place of summer
resort for the people of Rome; and in process
of time, when the city attained to an advanced
stage of opulence and luxury, the Roman
noblemen built villas there, choosing situations, in some instances, upon the natural ter-

races and esplanades of the promontory, which looked off over the sea, and in others cool and secluded retreats in the valleys, on the land. It was in one of these villas that Nero was born.

Nero's father belonged to a family which had enjoyed for several generations a considerable degree of distinction among the Roman nobility, though known by a somewhat whimsical name. The family name was Brazenbeard, or, to speak more exactly, it was Ahenobarbus, which is the Latin equivalent for that word. It is a question somewhat difficult to decide, whether in speaking of Nero's father at the present time, and in the English tongue, we should make use of the actual Latin name, or translate the word and employ the English representative of it; that is, whether we shall call him Ahenobarbus or Brazenbeard. The former seems to be more in harmony with our ideas of the dignity of Roman history; while the latter, though less elegant, conveys probably to our minds a more exact idea of the import and expression of the name as it sounded in the ears of the Roman community. The name certainly was not an attractive one, though the family had contriv-

ed to dignify it some degree by assigning to
it a preternatural origin. There was a tradi-
tion that in ancient times a prophet appeared
to one of the ancestors of the line, and after
foretelling certain extraordinary events which
were to occur at some future period, strok-
ed down the beard of his auditor with his
hand, and changed it to the color of brass,
in miraculous attestation of the divine authority of the message. The man received the
name of Brazenbeard in consequence, and he
and his descendants ever afterward retained
it.

The family of the Brazenbeards was one of
high rank and distinction, though at the time
of Nero's birth it was, like most of the other
prominent Roman families, extremely profligate and corrupt. Nero's father, especially,
was a very bad man. He was accused of the
very worst of crimes, and he led a life of constant remorse and terror. His wife, Agrippina, Nero's mother, was as wicked as he;
and it is said that when the messenger came
to him to announce the birth of his child, the
hero of this narrative, he uttered some excla-
mation of ill-humor and contempt, and said
that whatever came from him and Agrip

pina could not but be fraught with ruin to Rome.

The rank and station of Agrippina in Roman society was even higher than that of her husband. She was the sister of the emperor. The name of the emperor, her brother, was Caligula. He was the third in the series of Roman emperors, Augustus Cæsar, the successor of Julius Cæsar, having been the first. The term emperor, however, had a very different meaning in those days, from its present import. It seems to denote now a sovereign ruler, who exercises officially a general jurisdiction which extends over the whole government of the state. In the days of the Romans it included, in theory at least, only *military* command. The word was *imperator*, which meant *commander;* and the station which it denoted was simply that of general-in-chief over the military forces of the republic.

In the early periods of the Roman history, every possible precaution was taken to keep the military power in a condition of very strict subordination to the authority of the civil magistrate and of law. Very stringent regulations were adopted to secure this end. No

portion of the army, except such small de-
tachments as were required for preserving
order within the walls, was allowed to approach the city. Great commanders, in returning from their victorious campaigns, were
obliged to halt and encamp at some distance
from the gates, and there await the orders of
the Roman Senate. The *Senate* was, in theory, the great repository of political power.
This Senate was not, however, as the word
might seem in modern times to denote, a well-
defined and compact body of legislators, designated individually to the office, but rather a
class of hereditary nobles, very numerous, and
deriving their power from immemorial usage,
and from that strange and unaccountable
feeling of deference and awe with which the
mass of mankind always look up to an established, and especially an ancient, aristocracy.
The Senate were accustomed to convene at
stated times, in assemblages which were,
sometimes, conducted with a proper degree
of formality and order, and sometimes on the
other hand, exhibited scenes of great tumult
and confusion. Their power, however, whether
regularly or irregularly exercised, was supreme. They issued edicts, they enacted laws,

they alloted provinces, they made peace, and
they declared war. The armies, and the generals who commanded them, were the *agents*
employed to do their bidding.

The Roman armies consisted of vast bodies
of men which, when not in actual service,
were established in permanent encampments
in various parts of the empire, wherever it
was deemed necessary that troops should be
stationed. These great bodies of troops were
the celebrated Roman legions, and they were
renowned throughout the world for their discipline, their admirable organization, the
celerity of their movements, and for the in
domitable courage and energy of the men.
Each legion constituted, in fact, a separate
and independent community. Its camp was
its city. Its general was its king. In time
of war it moved, of course, from place to
place, as the exigencies of the service required; but in time of peace it established
itself with great formality in a spacious and
permanent encampment, which was laid out
with great regularity, and fortified with ram-
parts and fosses. Within the confines of the
camp the tents were arranged in rows, with
broad spaces for streets between them ; and

in a central position, before a space which served the purpose of a public square, the rich and ornamented pavilions of the commander and chief, and of the other generals, rose above the rest, like the public edifices of a city. The encampment of a Roman legion was, in fact, an extended and populous city, only that the dwellings consisted of tents instead of being formed of solid and permanent structures of wood or stone.

Roman legions were encamped in this way in various places throughout the empire, wherever the Senate thought proper to station them. There were some in Syria and the East; some in Italy; some on the banks of the Rhine; and it was through the instrumentality of the vast force thus organized, that the Romans held the whole European world under their sway. The troops were satisfied to yield submission to the orders of their commanders, since they received through them in return, an abundant supply of food and clothing, and lived, ordinarily, lives of ease and indulgence. In consideration of this, they were willing to march from place to place wherever they were ordered, and to fight any enemy when brought into the field

ENCAMPMENT OF A ROMAN LEGION.

LOSSING-BARRITT

2

The commanders obtained food and clothing
for them by means of the tribute which they
exacted from conquered provinces, and from
the plunder of sacked cities, in times of actual
war.   These armies were naturally interested
in preserving order and maintaining in general the authority of law, throughout the
communities which they controlled ; for without law and order the industrial pursuits of
men could not go on, and of course they were
well aware that if in any country production
were to cease, tribute must soon cease too.
In reading history we find, indeed, it must be
confessed, that a fearful proportion of the
narrative which describes the achievements
of ancient armies, is occupied with detailing
deeds of violence, rapine, and crime ; but we
must not infer from this that the influence of
these vast organizations was wholly evil.
Such extended and heterogeneous masses of
population as those which were spread over
Europe and Asia, in the days of the Romans,
could be kept subject to the necessary re
straints of social order only by some very
powerful instrumentality.   The legions organized by the Roman Senate, and stationed
here and there throughout the extended ter-

ritory, constituted this instrumentality. But
still, during far the greater portion of the
time the power which a legion wielded was
power in repose. It accomplished its end by
its simple presence, and by the sentiment of
awe which its presence inspired; and the na-
tions and tribes within the circle of its influence lived in peace, and pursued their industrial occupations without molestation, protect-
ed by the consciousness which everywhere
pervaded the minds of men, that the Roman
power was at hand. The legion hovered, as
it were, like a dark cloud in their horizon, silent and in repose; but containing, as they
well knew, the latent elements of thunder,
which might at any time burst upon their
heads. Thus, in its ordinary operation, its
influence was good. Occasionally and inci-
dentally periods of commotion would occur,
when its action was violent, cruel, and merci-
.essly evil. Unfortunately, however, for the
credit of the system in the opinion of mankind in subsequent ages, there was in the
good which it effected nothing to narrate;
while every deed of violence and crime which
was perpetrated by its agency, furnished ma
terials for an entertaining and exciting story

The good which was accomplished extended perhaps through a long, but monotonous period of quiescence and repose. The evil was brief, but was attended with a rapid succession of events, and varied by innumerable incidents ; so that the historian was accustomed to pass lightly over the one, with a few indifferent words of cold description, while he employed all the force of his genius in amplifying and adorning the narratives which commemorated the other. Thus, violent and oppressive as the military rulers were, by whom in ancient times the world was governed, they were less essentially and continuously violent and oppressive than the general tenor of history makes them seem ; and their crimes were, in some degree at least, compensated for and redeemed, by the really useful function which they generally fulfilled, of restraining and repressing all disorder and violence except their own.

The Roman legions, in particular, were for many centuries kept in tolerable subjection to the civil authorities of the capitol; but they were growing stronger and stronger all the time, and becoming more and more conscious of their strength. Every new com-

The progress of the military power.

mander who acquired renown by his victories
added greatly to the importance and influence of the army in its political relations.
The great Julius Cæsar, in the course of his
foreign conquests, and of his protracted and
terrible wars with Pompey, and with his
other rivals, made enormous strides in this
direction. Every time that he returned to
Rome at the head of his victorious legions,
he overawed the capitol more and more. Oc-
tavius Cæsar, the successor of Julius, known
generally in history by the name of Augustus,
completed what his uncle had begun. He
made the military authority, though still
nominally and in form subordinate, in reality
paramount and supreme. The Senate, indeed,
continued to assemble, and to exercise its
usual functions. Consuls and other civil magistrates were chosen, and invested with the
insignia of supreme command; and the customary forms and usages of civil administration, in which the subordination of the military to the civil power was fully recognized,
were all continued. Still, the actual authority of the civil government was wholly overawed and overpowered; and the haughty

imperator dictated to the Senate, and directed the administration, just as he pleased.

It required great genius in the commanders to bring up the army to this position of ascendency and power; but once up, it sustained itself there, without the necessity of ability of any kind, or of any lofty qualities whatever, in those subsequently placed at the head. In fact, the reader of history has often occasion to be perfectly amazed at the lengths to which human endurance will go, when a governmental power of any kind is once established, in tolerating imbecility and folly in the individual representatives of it. It seems to be immaterial whether the dominant power assumes the form of a dynasty of kings a class of hereditary nobles, or a line of military generals. It requires genius and statesmanship to instate it, but, once instated, no degree of stupidity, folly or crime in those who wield it, seems sufficient to exhaust the spirit of submission with which man always bows to established power—a spirit of submission which is so universal, and so patient and enduring, and which so transcends all the bounds of expediency and of reason, as to seem like a blind instinct implanted in the

very soul of man by the Author of his being—
a constituent and essential part of his nature
as a gregarious animal. In fact, without some
uch instinct, it would seem impossible that
Lose extended communities could be formed
and sustained, without which man, if he could
exist at all, could certainly never fully de
velop his capacities and powers.

However this may be in theory, it is cer
tain in fact, that the work of bringing up the
military power of ancient Rome to its condition of supremacy over all the civil functions
of government, was the work of men of the
most exalted capacities and powers. Marius
and Sylla, Pompey and Cæsar, Antony and
Augustus, evinced, in all their deeds, a high
degree of sagacity, energy, and greatness of
soul. Mankind, though they may condemn
their vices and crimes, will never cease to
admire the grandeur of their ambition, and
the magnificence, comprehensiveness, and ef-
ficiency of their plans of action. The whole
known world was the theater of their con-
ests, and the armies which they organized
and disciplined, and which they succeeded at
length in bringing under the control of one
central and consolidated command, formed

the most extended and imposing military
power that the world had ever seen. It was
not only vast in extent, but permanent and
self-sustaining in character. A wide and
complicated, but most effectual system was
adopted for maintaining it. Its discipline
was perfect. Its organization was complete.
It was equally trained to remain quietly at
home in its city-like encampments, in time of
peace, or to march, or bivouac, or fight, in
time of war. Such a system could be formed
only by men possessed of mental powers of
the highest character; but, once formed, it
could afterward sustain itself; and not only
so, but it was found capable of holding up,
by its own inherent power, the most imbecile
and incompetent men, as the nominal rulers
of it.

Caligula, for example, the brother of Agrippina, and the reigning emperor at the time
of Nero's birth, was a man wholly unfit to
exercise any high command. He was ele
vated to the post by the influence of the army,
simply because he was the most prominent
man among those who had hereditary claims
to the succession, and was thus the man whom
the army could most easily place in the office

of chieftain, and retain most securely there
His life, however, in the lofty station to which
accident thus raised him, was one of continual
folly, vice and crime. He lived generally at
Rome, where he expended the immense revenues that were at his command in the most
wanton and senseless extravagance. In the
earlier part of his career the object of much
of his extravagance was the gratification of
the people; but after a time he began to seek
only gratifications for himself, and at length
he evinced the most wanton spirit of malignity and cruelty toward others. He seemed
at last actually to hate the whole human species, and to take pleasure in teasing and tormenting men, whenever an occasion of any
kind occurred to afford him the opportunity.
They were accustomed in those days to have
spectacles and shows in vast amphitheaters
which were covered, when the sun was hot,
with awnings. Sometimes when an amphi-
theater was crowded with spectators, and the
heat of the sun was unusually powerful, Caligula would order the awnings to be removed
and the doors to be kept closed so as to prevent the egress of the people; and then he
would amuse himself with the indications of

discomfort and suffering which so crowded a concourse in such an exposure would necessarily exhibit. He kept wild animals for the combats which took place in these amphitheaters, and when it was difficult to procure the flesh of sheep and oxen for them, he would feed them with men, throwing into their dens for this purpose criminals and captives. Some persons who offended him, he ordered to be branded in the face with hot irons, by which means they were not only subjected to cruel torture at the time, but were frightfully disfigured for life. Sometimes when the sons of noble or distinguished men displeased him, or when under the influence of his caprice or malignity he conceived some feeling of hatred toward them, he would order them to be publicly executed, and he would require their parents to be present and witness the scene. At one time after such an execution he required the wretched father of his victim to come and sup with him at his palace; and while at supper he talked with his guest all the time, in a light, and jocular, and mirthful manner, in order to trifle with and insult the mental anguish of the sufferer. At another time when he had commanded a distinguished

senator to be present at the execution of his
son, the senator said that he would go, in obedience to the emperor's orders, but humbly
asked permission to shut his eyes at the moment of the execution, that he might be spared
the dreadful anguish of witnessing the dying
struggles of his son. The emperor in reply
immediately condemned the father to death
for daring to make so audacious a proposal.

Of course the connection of Agrippina, the
mother of Nero, with such a sovereign as this,
while it gave her a very high social position
in the Roman community, could not contrib-
ute much to her happiness. In fact all who
were connected with Caligula in any way
lived in continual terror, for so wanton and
capricious was his cruelty, that all who were
liable to come under his notice at all were
in constant danger. Agrippina herself at
one time incurred her brother's displeasure,
though she was fortunate enough to escape
with her life. Caligula discovered, or pretended to discover, a conspiracy against him,
and he accused Agrippina and another of his
sisters named Livilla of being implicated in
it. Caligula sent a soldier to the leader of
the conspiracy to cut off his head, and then

he banished his sisters from Rome and shut them up in the island of Pontia, telling them when they went away, to beware, for he had swords for them as well as islands, in case of need.

At length Caligula's terrible tyranny was brought to a sudden end by his assassination; and Agrippina, in consequence of this event was not only released from her thraldom but raised to a still higher eminence than she had enjoyed before. The circumstances connected with these events will be related in the next chapter.

15—3

CHAPTER II.

THE ASSASSINATION OF CALIGULA

THE emperor Caligula came to his death in the following manner:

Of course his wanton and remorseless tyranny often awakened very deep feelings of resentment, and very earnest desires for revenge in the hearts of those who suffered by it; but yet so absolute and terrible was his power, that none dared to murmur or complain. The resentment, however, which the cruelty of the emperor awakened, burned the more fiercely for being thus restrained and suppressed, and many covert threats were made, and many secret plots were formed, from time to time, against the tyrant's life.

Among others who cherished such designs, there was a man named Cassius Chærea, an officer of the army, who, though not of high rank, was nevertheless a man of considerable distinction. He was a captain, or, as it was styled in those days, a centurion. His command, therefore, was small, but it was in the

prætorian cohort, as it was called, a sort of
body-guard of the commander-in-chief, and
consequently a very honorable corps. Chærea
was thus a man of considerable distinction on
account of the post which he occupied, and
his duties, as captain in the life guards,
brought him very frequently into communication with the emperor. He was a man of
great personal bravery, too, and was on this
account held in high consideration by the
army. He had performed an exploit at one
time, some years before, in Germany, which
had gained him great fame. It was at the
time of the death of Augustus, the first emperor. Some of the German legions, and
among them one in which Chærea was serv-
ing, had seized upon the occasion to revolt
They alledged many and grievous acts of oppression as the grounds of their revolt, and
demanded redress for what they had suffered,
and security for the future. One of the first
measures which they resorted to in the frenzy
of the first outbreak of the rebellion, was to
seize all the centurions in the camp, and to
beat them almost to death. They gave them
sixty blows each, one for each of their num
ber, and then turned them, bruised, wounded

and dying, out of the camp. Some they threw into the Rhine. They revenged themselves thus on all the centurions but one. That one was Chærea. Chærea would not suffer himself to be taken by them, but seizing his sword he fought his way through the midst of them, slaying some and driving others before him, and thus made his escape from the camp. This feat gained him great renown.

One might imagine from this account that Chærea was a man of great personal superiority in respect to size and strength, inasmuch as extraordinary muscular power, as well as undaunted courage, would seem to be required to enable a man to make his way against so many enemies. But this was not the fact. Chærea was of small stature and of a slender and delicate form. He was modest and unassuming in his manners, too, and of a very kind and gentle spirit. He was thus not only honored and admired for his courage, but he was generally beloved for the amiable and excellent qualities of his heart.

The possession of such qualities, however, could not be expected to recommend him par ticularly to the favor of the emperor. In fact, in one instance it had the contrary effect. Caligula assigned to the centurions of his guard, at one period, some duties connected with the collection of taxes. Chærea, instead of practicing the extortion and cruelty common on such occasions, was merciful and considerate, and governed himself strictly by the rules of law and of justice in his collections. The consequence necessarily was that the amount of money received was somewhat diminished, and the emperor was displeased. The occasion was, however, not one of sufficient importance to awaken in the monarch's mind any very serious anger, and so, instead of inflicting any heavy punishment upon the offender, he contented himself with attempting to tease and torment him with sundry vexatious indignities and annoyances.

It is the custom sometimes, in camps, and at other military stations, for the commander to give every evening, what is called the *parole* or password, which consists usually of some word or phrase that is to be communicated to all the officers, and as occasion may require to all the soldiers, whom for any reason it may be necessary to send to and fro

3

about the precincts of the camp during the night. The sentinels, also, all have the password, and accordingly, whenever any man approaches the post of a sentinel, he is stopped and the parole is demanded. If the stranger gives it correctly, it is presumed that all is right, and he is allowed to pass on,— since an enemy or a spy would have no means of knowing it.

Now, whenever it came to Chærea's turn to communicate the parole, the emperor was accustomed to give him some ridiculous or indecent phrase, intended not only to be offensive to the purity of Chærea's mind, but designed, also, to exhibit him in a ridiculous light to the subordinate officers and soldiers to whom he would have to communicate it. Sometimes the password thus given was some word or phrase wholly unfit to be spoken, and sometimes it was the name of some notorious and infamous woman ; but whatever it was, Chærea was compelled by his duty as a soldier to deliver it to all the corps, and patiently to submit to the laughter and derision which his communication awakened among the vile and wicked soldiery.

If there was any dreadful punishment to be

inflicted, or cruel deed of any kind to be performed, Caligula took great pleasure in assigning the duty to Chærea, knowing how ab-
horrent to his nature it must be. At one time
a senator of great distinction named Propedius, was accused of treason by one of his
enemies. His treason consisted, as the accuser alledged, of having spoken injurious
words against the emperor. Propedius denied that he had ever spoken such words.
The accuser, whose name was Timidius, cited
a certain Quintilia, an actress, as his witness.
Propedius was accordingly brought to trial,
and Quintilia was called upon before the
judges to give her testimony. She denied
that she had ever heard Propedius utter any
such sentiment as Timidius attributed to him.
Timidius then said that Quintilia was testify-
ing falsely: he declared that she had heard
Propedius utter such words, and demanded
that she should be put to the torture to compel her to acknowledge it. The emperor
acceded to this demand, and commanded
Chærea to put the actress to the torture.

It is, of course, always difficult to ascertain
the precise truth in respect to such transac
tions as those that are connected with plots

and conspiracies against tyrants, since every
possible precaution is, of course, taken by all
concerned to conceal what is done. It is probable, however, in this case, that Propedius had
cherished some hostile designs against Caligula, if he had not uttered injurious words,
and that Quintilia was in some measure in
his confidence. It is even possible that Chærea may have been connected with them in
some secret design, for it is said that when he
received the orders of Caligula to put Quintilia to the torture he was greatly agitated and
alarmed. If he should apply the torture se-
verely, he feared that the unhappy sufferer
might be induced to make confessions or
statements at least, which would bring destruction on the men whom he most relied
upon for the overthrow of Caligula. On the
other hand, if he should attempt to spare her,
the effect would be only to provoke the anger
of Caligula against himself, without at all
shielding or saving her. As, however, he was
proceeding to the place of torture, in charge
of his victim, with his mind in this state of
anxiety and indecision, his fears were somewhat relieved by a private signal given to
him by Quintilia, by which she intimated to

him that he need feel no concern,—that she would be faithful and true, and would re veal nothing, whatever might be done to her.

This assurance, while it allayed in some degree Chærea's anxieties and fears, must have greatly increased the mental distress which he endured at the idea of leading such a woman to the awful suffering which awaited her. He could not, however, do otherwise than to proceed. Having arrived at the place of execution, the wretched Quintilia was put to the rack. She bore the agony which she endured while her limbs were stretched on the torturing engine, and her bones broken, with patient submission, to the end. She was then carried, fainting, helpless, and almost dead, to Caligula, who seemed now satisfied. He ordered the unhappy victim of the torture to be taken away, and directed that Prope-dius should be acquitted and discharged.

Of course while passing through this scene the mind of Chærea was in a tumult of agita-tion and excitement,—the anguish of mind which he must have felt in his compassion for the sufferer, mingling and contending with the desperate indignation which burned in his bosom against the author of all these mis-

42 NERO. [A.D. 40

Anger of Chærea. His determination to destroy Caligula.

eries. He was wrought up, in fact, to such a
state of frenzy by this transaction, that as soon
as it was over he determined immediately to
take measures to put Caligula to death. This
was a very bold and desperate resolution.
Caligula was the greatest and most powerful
potentate on earth. Chærea was only a captain of his guard, without any political influence or power, and with no means whatever
of screening himself from the terrible consequences which might be expected to follow
from his attempt, whether it should succeed
or fail.

So thoroughly, however, was he now aroused, that he determined to brave every danger
in the attainment of his end. He immediately
began to seek out among the officers of the
army such men as he supposed would be most
likely to join him,—men of courage, resolution, and faithfulness, and those who, from
their general character or from the wrongs
which they had individually endured from
the government, were to be supposed specially
hostile to Caligula's dominion. From among
these men he selected a few, and to them he
cautiously unfolded his designs. All approved
of them. Some, it is true, declined taking

any active part in the conspiracy, but they assured Chærea of their good wishes, and promised solemnly not to betray him.

The number of the conspirators daily increased. There was, however, at their meetings for consultation, some difference of opinion in respect to the course to be pursued. Some were in favor of acting promptly and at once. The greatest danger which was to be apprehended, they thought, was in delay. As the conspiracy became extended, some one would at length come to the knowledge of it, they said, who would betray them. Others, on the other hand, were for proceeding cautiously and slowly. What they most feared was rash and inconsiderate action. It would be ruinous to the enterprise, as they maintained, for them to attempt to act before their plans were fully matured.

Chærea was of the former opinion. He was very impatient to have the deed performed. He was ready himself, he said, to perform it, at any time ; his personal duties as an officer of the guard, gave him frequent occasions of access to the emperor, and he was ready to avail himself of any of them to kill the monster. The emperor went often, he said, to the

capitol, to offer sacrifices, and he could easily
kill him there. Or, if they thought that that
was too public an occasion, he could have an
opportunity in the palace, at certain religious
ceremonies which the emperor was accustomed to perform there, and at which Chærea
himself was usually present. Or, he was
ready to throw him down from a tower where
he was accustomed to go sometimes for the
purpose of scattering money among the popu
lace below. Chærea said that he could easily
come up behind him on such an occasion, and
hurl him suddenly over the parapet down to
the pavement below. All these plans, however, seemed to the conspirators too uncertain
and dangerous, and Chærea's proposals were
accordingly not agreed to.

At length, the time drew near when Caligula was to leave Rome to proceed to Alexan-
dria in Egypt, and the conspirators perceived
that they must prepare to act, or else abandon their design altogether. It had been
arranged that there was to be a grand celebration at Rome previous to the emperor's
departure. This celebration, which was to
consist of games, and sports, and dramatic
performances of various kinds, was to con

tinue for three days, and the conspirators determined, after much consultation and debate, that Caligula should be assassinated on one of those days.

After coming to this conclusion, however, in general, their hearts seemed to fail them in fixing the precise time for the perpetration of the deed, and two of the three days passed away accordingly without any attempt being made. At length, on the morning of the third day, Chærea called the chief conspirators together, and urged them very earnestly not to let the present opportunity pass away. He represented to them how greatly they increased the danger of their attempts by such delays, and he seemed himself so full of determination and courage, and addressed them with so much eloquence and power, that he inspired them with his own resolution, and they decided unanimously to proceed.

The emperor came to the theater that day at an unusually early hour, and seemed to be in excellent spirits and in an excellent humor. He was very complaisant to all around him, and very lively, affable, and gay. After performing certain ceremonies, by which it devolved upon him to open the festivities of the

day, he proceeded to his place, with his
friends and favorites about him, and Chærea,
with the other officers that day on guard, at a
little distance behind him.

The performances were commenced, and
every thing went on as usual until toward
noon. The conspirators kept their plans pro-
foundly secret, except that one of them, when
he had taken his seat by the side of a distinguished senator, asked him whether he had
heard any thing new. The senator replied
that he had not. "I can then tell you something," said he, "which perhaps you have
not heard, and that is, that in the piece which
is to be acted to-day, there is to be represented the death of a tyrant." "Hush!" said
the senator, and he quoted a verse from Ho-
mer, which meant, "Be silent, lest some Greek
should overhear."

It had been the usual custom of the emperor,
at such entertainments, to take a little recess
about noon, for rest and refreshments. It
devolved upon Chærea to wait upon him at
this time, and to conduct him from his place
in the theater to an adjoining apartment in
his palace which was connected with the
theater, where there was provided a bath and

various refreshments. When the time arrived, and Chærea perceived, as he thought, that the emperor was about to go, he himself went out, and stationed himself in a passageway leading to the bath, intending to intercept and assassinate the emperor when he should come along. The emperor, however, delayed his departure, having fallen into conversation with his courtiers and friends, and finally he said that, on the whole, as it was the last day of the festival, he would not go out to the bath, but would remain in the theater; and then ordering refreshments to be brought to him there, he proceeded to distribute them with great urbanity to the officers around him.

In the mean time, Chærea was patiently waiting in the passage-way, with his sword by his side, all ready for striking the blow the moment that his victim should appear. Of course the conspirators who remained behind were in a state of great suspense and anxiety, and one of them, named Minucianus, determined to go out and inform Chærea of the change in Caligula's plans. He accordingly attempted to rise, but Caligula put his hand upon his robe, saying, "Sit still, my

friend. You shall go with me presently.'
Minucianus accordingly dissembled his anxiety and agitation of mind still a little longer,
but presently, watching an opportunity when
the emperor's attention was otherwise engaged, he rose, and, assuming an unconcerned
and careless air, he walked out of the theater.

He found Chærea in his ambuscade in the
passage-way, and he immediately informed
him that the emperor had concluded not to
come out. Chærea and Minucianus were
then greatly at a loss what to do. Some of
the other conspirators, who had followed
Minucianus out, now joined them, and a brief
but very earnest and solemn consultation ensued. After a moment's hesitation, Chærea
declared that they must now go through with
their work at all hazards, and he professed
himself ready, if his comrades would sustain
him in it, to go back to the theater, and stab
the tyrant there in his seat, in the midst of
his friends. Minucianus and the others con-
curred in this design, and it was resolved
immediately to execute it.

The execution of the plan, however, in the
precise form in which it had been resolved
upon was prevented by a new turn which af

fairs had taken in the theater. For while Minucianus and the two or three conspirators who had accompanied him were debating in the passage-way, the others who remained, knowing that Chærea was expecting Caligula to go out, conceived the idea of attempting to persuade him to go, and thus to lead him into the snare which had been set for him. They accordingly gathered around, and without any appearance of concert or of eagerness, began to recommend him to go and take his bath as usual. He seemed at length disposed to yield to these persuasions, and rose from his seat; and then, the whole company attending and following him, he proceeded toward the doors which conducted to the palace. The conspirators went before him, and under pretense of clearing the way for him they contrived to remove to a little distance all whom they thought would be most disposed to render him any assistance. The consultations of Chærea and those who were with him in the inner passage-way were interrupted by the coming of this company.

Among those who walked with the emperor at this time were his uncle Claudius and other distinguished relatives. Caligula advanced

along the passage, walking in company with
these friends, and wholly unconscious of the
fate that awaited him, but instead of going
immediately toward the bath he turned aside
first into a gallery or corridor which led into
another apartment, where there were assembled a company of boys and girls, that had
been sent to him from Asia to act and dance
upon the stage, and who had just arrived.
The emperor took great interest in looking at
these performers, and seemed desirous of having them go immediately into the theater and
let him see them perform.   While talking on
this subject Chærea and the other conspirators
came into the apartment, determined now to
strike the blow.

Chærea advanced to the emperor, and
asked him in the usual manner what should
be the parole for that night. The emperor
gave him in reply such an one as he had often
chosen before, to insult and degrade him.
Chærea instead of receiving the insult meekly
and patiently in his usual manner, uttered
words of anger and defiance in reply; and
drawing his sword at the same instant he
struck the emperor across the neck and felled
him to the floor.   Caligula filled the apart

ment with his cries of pain and terror; the other conspirators rushed in and attacked him on all sides; his friends,—so far as the adherents of such a man can be called friends,—fled in dismay. As for Caligula's uncle Claudius, it was not to have been expected that he would have rendered his nephew any aid, for he was a man of such extraordinary mental imbecility that he was usually considered as not possessed even of common sense; and all the others who might have been expected to defend him, either fled from the scene, or stood by in consternation and amazement, leaving the conspirators to wreak their vengeance on their wretched victim, to the full.

In fact though while a despot lives and retains his power, thousands are ready to defend him and to execute his will, however much in heart they may hate and detest him, yet when he is dead, or when it is once certain that he is about to die, an instantaneous change takes place and every one turns against him. The multitudes in and around the theater and the palace who had an hour before trembled before this mighty potentate, and seemed to live only to do his bidding, were filled with joy to see him brought to the

dust. The conspirators, when the success of
their plans and the death of their oppressor
was once certain, abandoned themselves to
the most extravagant joy. They cut and
stabbed the fallen body again and again, as
if they could never enough wreak their ven
geance upon it. They cut off pieces of the
body and bit them with their teeth in their
savage exultation and triumph. At length
they left the body where it lay, and went forth
into the city where all was now of course tumult and confusion.

The body remained where it had fallen until late at night. Then some attendants of
the palace came and conveyed it away. They
were sent, it was said, by Cæsonia, the wife
of the murdered man. Cæsonia had an infant
daughter at this time, and she remained herself with the child, in a retired apartment of
the palace while these things were transpir-
ing. Distracted with grief and terror at the
tidings that she heard, she clung to her babe,
and made the arrangements for the interment
of the body of her husband without leaving
its cradle. She imagined perhaps that there
was no reason for supposing that she or the
child were in any immediate danger, and ac

CÆSONIA.

cordingly she took no measures toward effecting an escape. If so, she did not understand the terrible frenzy to which the conspirators had been aroused, and for which the
long series of cruelties and indignities which
they had endured from her husband had prepared them. For at midnight one of them
broke into her apartment, stabbed the mother
in her chair, and taking the innocent infant
from its cradle, killed it by beating its head
against the wall.

Atrocious as this deed may seem, it was not altogether wanton and malignant cruelty which prompted it. The conspirators intended by the assassination of Caligula not merely to wreak their vengeance on a single man, but to bring to an end a hated race of tyrants ; and they justified the murder of the wife and child by the plea that stern political necessity required them to exterminate the line, in order that no successor might subsequently arise to re-establish the power and renew the tyranny which they had brought to an end. The history of monarchies is continually presenting us with instances of innocent and helpless children sacrificed to such a supposed necessity as this.

CHAPTER III.

THE ACCESSION OF CLAUDIUS.

IN the assassination of Caligula, the con
spirators who combined to perpetrate
the deed, had a much deeper design than that
of merely gratifying their personal resentment and rage against an individual tyrant.
They wished to effect a permanent change in
the government, by putting down the army
from the position of supreme and despotic
authority which it had assumed, and restoring the dominion to the Roman Senate, and
to the other civil authorities of the city, as it
had been exercised by them in former years.
Of course, the death of Caligula was the commencement, not the end, of the great struggle.
The whole country was immediately divided
into two parties. There was the party of the
Senate, and the party of the army; and a
long and bitter conflict ensued. It was for
some time doubtful which would win the
day.

In fact, immediately after Caligula was

killed, and the tidings of his death began to
spread about the palace and into the streets
of the city, a considerable tumult arose, the
precursor and earnest of the dissensions that
were to follow.   Upon the first alarm, a body
of the emperor's guards that had been accustomed to attend upon his person, and whom
he had strongly attached to himself by his
lavish generosity in bestowing presents and
rewards upon them, rushed forward to defend
him, or if it should prove too late to defend
him, to avenge his death.   These soldiers ran
toward the palace, and when they found that
the emperor had been killed, they were furi
ous with rage, and fell upon all whom they
met, and actually slew several men.   Tid
ings came to the theater, and the word was
spread from rank to rank among the people
that the emperor was slain.   The people did
not, however, at first, believe the story.   They
supposed that the report was a cunning contrivance of the emperor himself, intended to
entrap them into some expression of pleasure
and gratification, on their part, at his death,
in order to give him an excuse for inflicting
some cruel punishment upon them.   The noise
and tumult in the streets soon convinced them.

however, that something extraordinary had occurred; they learned that the news of the emperor's death was really true, and almost immediately afterward they found, to their consternation, that the furious guards were thundering at the gates of the theater, and endeavoring to force their way in, in order to wreak their vengeance on the assembly, as if the spectators at the show were accomplices of the crime.

In the mean time Chærea and the other chief conspirators had fled to a secret place of retreat, where they now lay concealed. As soon as they had found that the object of their vengeance was really dead, and when they had satisfied themselves with the pleasure of cutting and stabbing the lifeless body, they stole away to the house of one of their friends in the neighborhood, where they could lie for a time secreted in safety. The life-guards sought for them everywhere, but could not find them. The streets were filled with tumult and confusion. Rumors of every kind, false and true, spread in all directions, and increased the excitement. At length, however, the consuls, who were the chief magistrates of the republic, succeeded in organiz

ing a force and in restoring order. They took
possession of the forum and of the capitol,
and posted sentinels and guards along the
streets. They compelled the emperor's guards
to desist from their violence, and retire. They
sent a herald clothed in mourning into the
theater, to announce officially to the people
the event which had occurred, and to direct
them to repair quietly to their homes. Having taken these preliminary measures they
immediately called the Senate together, to
deliberate on the emergency which had occurred, and to decide what should next be
done. In the mean time the emperor's guards,
having withdrawn from the streets of the city,
retired to their camp and joined their comrades. Thus there were two vast powers
organized—that of the army in the camp, and
that of the Senate in the city—each jealous
of the other, and resolute in its determination
not to yield, in the approaching conflict.

In times of sudden and violent revolution
like that which attended the death of Caligula,
the course which public affairs are to take,
and the question who is to rise and who is to
fall, seem often to be decided by utter accident. It was strikingly so in this instance, in

respect to the selection, on the part of the
army, of the man who was to take the post of
supreme command in the place of the murdered emperor. The choice fell on Claudius,
Agrippina's uncle. It fell upon him, too, as
it would seem, by the merest chance, in the
following very extraordinary manner.

Claudius, as has already been said, was
Caligula's uncle; and as Caligula and Agrippina were brother and sister, he was, of course,
Agrippina's uncle too. He was at this time
about fifty years of age, and he was universally ridiculed and contemned on account of
his great mental and personal inferiority. He
was weak and ill-formed at his birth, so that
even his mother despised him. She called
him "an unfinished little monster," and whenever she wished to express her contempt for
any one in respect to his understanding, she
used to say, "You are as stupid as my son
Claudius." In a word, Claudius was extremely unfortunate in every respect, so far as
natural endowments are concerned. His
countenance was very repulsive, his figure was
ungainly, his manners were awkward, his
voice was disagreeable, and he had an impediment in his speech. In fact, he was consid-

60   NERO.   [A.D. 41.

Every one against him.   Mode of teasing him.

ered in his youth as almost an idiot. He was
not allowed to associate with the other Roman
boys of his age, but was kept apart, in some
secluded portion of the palace, with women
and slaves, where he was treated with so much
cruelty and neglect that what little spirit nature had given him was crushed and destroyed. In fact, by common consent all seemed
to take pleasure in teasing and tormenting
him. Sometimes, when he was coming to the
table at an entertainment, the other guests
would combine to exclude him from the seats,
in order to enjoy his distress as he ran about
from one part of the table to another, endeav
oring to find a place. If they found him
asleep they would pelt him with olives and
dates, or awaken him with the blow of a rod
or a whip; and sometimes they would stealthily put his sandals upon his hands while he
was asleep, in order that when he awoke suddenly they might amuse themselves with seeing him rub his face and eyes with them.

After all, however, the inferiority of Claudius was not really so great as it seemed. He
was awkward and ungainly, no doubt, to the
last degree; but he possessed some considerable capacity for intellectual pursuits and at

tainments, and as he was pretty effectually driven away from society by the jests and ridicule to which he was subjected, he devoted a great deal of time in his retirement to study, and to other useful pursuits. He made considerable progress in the efforts which he thus made to cultivate his mind. He, however, failed to acquire the respect of those around him; and as he grew up he seemed to be considered utterly incapable of performing any useful function; and during the time when his nephew Caligula was emperor, he remained at court, among the other nobles, but still neglected and despised by all of them. It is said that he probably owed the preservation of his life to his insignificance, as Caligula would probably have found some pretext for destroying him, if he had not thought him too spiritless and imbecile to form any ambitious plans. In fact, Claudius said himself afterward, when he became emperor, that a great part of his apparent simplicity was feigned, as a measure of prudence, to protect himself from injury. When Claudius grew up he was married several times. The wife who was living with him at the time of Caligula's death was his third wife: hei

name was Valeria Messalina. She was his
cousin. Claudius and Messalina had one
child—a daughter, named Octavia. Claudius
had been extremely unhappy in his connection with the wives preceding Messalina. He
had quarreled with them and been divorced
from them both. He had had a daughter by
one of these wives and a son by the other.
The son was suddenly killed by getting choked
with a small pear. He had been throwing it
into the air and attempting to catch it in his
mouth as it came down, when at last it slipped
down into his throat and strangled him. As
for the daughter, Claudius was so exasperated
with her mother at the time of his divorce
from her, that he determined to disown and
reject the child ; so he ordered the terrified
girl to be stripped naked, and to be sent and
laid down in that condition at her wretched
mother's door.

Claudius, as has already been stated, was
present with Caligula at the theater, on the
last day of the spectacle, and followed him
into the palace when he went to look at the
Asiatic captives ; so that he was present, or at
least very near, at the time of his nephew's
assassination. As might have been expected

from what has been said of his character, he
was overwhelmed with consternation and ter
ror a the scene, and was utterly incapacitated
from taking any part, either for or against the
conspirators. He stole away in great fright
and hid himself behind the hangings in a dark
recess in the palace. Here he remained for
some time, listening in an agony of anxiety
and suspense to the sounds which he heard
around him. He could hear the cries and the
tumult in the streets, and in the passages of
the palace. Parties of the guards, in going
to and fro, passed by the place of his retreat
from time to time, alarming him with the
clangor of their weapons, and their furious
exclamations and outcries. At one time peep-
ing stealthily out, he saw a group of soldiers
hurrying along with a bleeding head on the
point of a pike. It was the head of a prominent citizen of Rome whom the guards had
intercepted and killed, supposing him to be
one of the conspirators. This spectacle greatly
increased Claudius's terror. He was wholly
in the dark in respect to the motives and the
designs of the men who had thus revolted
against his nephew, and it was of course im
possible for him to know how he himself

He is discovered by a soldier.

would be regarded by either party. He did
not dare, therefore, to surrender himself to
either, but remained in his concealment, suffering great anxiety, and utterly unable to decide what to do.

At length, while he was in this situation of
uncertainty and terror, a common soldier of
the guards, named Epirius, who happened to
pass that way, accidentally saw his feet beneath the hangings, and immediately, pulling

DISCOVERY OF CLAUDIUS.

the hangings aside, dragged him out to view.
Claudius supposed now, of course, that his
hour was come. He fell on his knees in an
agony of terror, and begged the soldier to
spare his life. The soldier, when he found
that his prisoner was Claudius, the uncle of
Caligula, raised him from the ground and sa-
luted him emperor. As Caligula left no son,
Epirius considered Claudius as his nearest
relative, and consequently as the heir. Epirius immediately summoned others of the
guard to the place, saying that he had found
the new emperor, and calling upon them to
assist in conveying him to the camp. The
soldiers thus summoned procured a chair, and
having placed the astonished Claudius in it,
they raised the chair upon their shoulders, and
began to convey it away. As they bore him
thus along the streets, the people who saw
them supposed that they were taking him to
execution, and they lamented his unhappy
fate. Claudius himself knew not what to believe. He could not but hope that his life
was to be saved, but then he could not wholly
dispel his fears.

In the mean time, the soldiers went steadily
forward with their burden. When one set of

bearers became fatigued, they set down the chair, and others relieved them. No one molested them, or attempted to intercept them in their progress, and at length they reached the camp. Claudius was well received by the whole body of the army. The officers held a consultation that night, and determined to make him emperor. At first he was extremely unwilling to accept the proffered honor, but they urged it upon him, and he was at length induced to accept it. Thus the army was once more provided with a head, and prepared to engage anew in its conflict with the civil authorities of the city.

The particulars of the conflict that ensued we can not here describe. It is sufficient to say that the army prevailed, and that Claudius soon found himself in full possession of the power from which his nephew had been so suddenly deposed.

One of the first measures which the new emperor adopted, was to recall Agrippina from her banishment at Pontia, where Caligula had confined her, and restore her to her former position in Rome. Her husband, Brazenbeard, died about this time, and young Brazenbeard, her son, afterward called Nero,

the subject of this history, was three years
old. Octavia, the daughter of Claudius and
Messalina, was a little younger.

Messalina, the wife of Claudius, hated
Agrippina, considering her, as she did, her
rival and enemy. The favor which Claudius
showed to Agrippina, in recalling her from
her banishment, and treating her with consideration and favor at Rome, only inflamed
still more Messalina's hatred. She could not,
however, succeed in inducing Claudius to
withdraw his protection from his niece; for
Claudius, though almost entirely subject to
the influence and control of his wife in most
things, seemed fully determined not to yield
to her wishes in this. Agrippina continued,
therefore, to live at Rome, in high favor with
the court, for several years,—her little son
advancing all the time in age and in maturity, until at length he became twelve years
old. At this time, another great change took
place in his own and his mother's condition.
Messalina became herself, by her wickedness
and infatuation, the means of raising her rival
into her own place as wife of the emperor.
The result was accomplished in the following
manner.

Messalina had long been a very dissolute and wicked woman, having been accustomed to give herself up to criminal indulgences and pleasures of every kind, in company with favorites whom she selected from time to time among the courtiers around her. For a time she managed these intrigues with some degree of caution and secrecy, in order to conceal her conduct from her husband. She gradually, however, became more and more open and bold. She possessed a great ascendency over the mind of her husband, and could easily deceive him, or induce him to do whatever she pleased. She persuaded him to confer honors and rewards in a very liberal manner upon those whom she favored, and to degrade, and sometimes even to destroy, those who displeased her. She would occasionally resort to very cunning artifices to accomplish her ends. For example, she conceived at one time a violent hatred against the husband of her mother. His name was Silanus. He was not the father of Messalina, but a second husband of Messalina's mother; and, being young and attractive in person, Messalina at first loved him, and intended to make him one of her favorites and compan-

ions.   Silanus, however, would not accede to
her wishes, and her love for him was then
changed into hatred and thirst for revenge.
She accordingly determined on his destruction; but as she knew that it would be difficult to induce Claudius to proceed to extremities against him, on account of his intimate
relationship to the family, she contrived a
very artful plot to accomplish her ends   It
was this:

She sent word to Silanus, on a certain evening, that the emperor wished him to come
to the palace, to his private apartment, the
next morning, at a very early hour.   The emperor wished to see him, the messenger said,
on business of importance.

Just before the time which had been appointed for Silanus to appear, a certain officer
of the household, named Narcissus, whom
Messalina had engaged to assist her in her
plot, came into the emperor's apartment, with
an anxious countenance, and in a very hurried manner, and said to Claudius, whom he
waked out of sleep by his coming, that he
had had a very frightful dream—one which
he deemed it his duty to make known to his
master without any delay.   He dreamed, he

said, that a plot had been formed for assassinating the emperor; that Silanus was the contriver of it, and that he was coming early that morning to carry his design into effect. Messalina, who was present with her husband at the time, listened to this story with well-feigned anxiety and agitation, and then declared, with a countenance of great mysteriousness and solemnity, that she had had precisely the same dream for two or three nights in succession, but that, not being willing to do Silanus an injury, or to raise any unjust suspicions against him, she had thus far forborne to speak of the subject to her husband. She was, however, now convinced, she said, that Silanus was really entertaining some treasonable designs, and that the dreams were tokens sent from heaven to warn the emperor of his danger.

Claudius, who was of an extremely timid and nervous temperament, was very much alarmed by these communications; and his terrors were greatly increased by the appearance of a servant who announced to him at that moment that Silanus was then coming in. The coming of Silanus to the palace at that unseasonable hour was considered by the em

peror as full confirmation of the dreams which
had been related to him, and as proof of the
guilt of the accused; and under the impulse
of the sudden passion and fear which this conviction awakened in his mind, he ordered
Silanus to be seized and led away to immediate execution. These commands were
obeyed. Silanus was hurried away and dispatched by the swords of the soldiers, without
ever knowing what the accusation was that
had been made against him.

Thus Messalina succeeded by artifice and
cunning in accomplishing her ends, in cases
where she could not rely on her direct influence upon the mind of the emperor. In one
way or the other she almost always effected
whatever she undertook, and gradually came
to exercise almost supreme control. Whom
she would she raised up, and whom she would
she put down. In the mean time she lived
herself, a life of the most guilty indulgence
and pleasure. For a long time she concealed
her wickedness from the emperor. He was
very easily deceived, and though Messalina's
character was perfectly well known to others,
he himself continued blind to her guilt. At
length, however, she began to grow more and

more bold. She became satiated, as one of her
historians says of her, with the common and
ordinary forms of vice, and wished for something new and unusual to give piquancy and
life to her sensations. At length, however, she
went one step too far, and brought upon herself in consequence of it a terrible destruction.

It was about seven years after the accession
of Claudius that the event occurred. The favorite of Messalina at this time was a young
Roman senator named Caius Silius. Silius
was a very distinguished young nobleman,
and a man of handsome person and of very
graceful and accomplished manners and address. He was in fact a very general favorite, and Messalina, when she first saw him,
conceived a very strong affection for him.
He was, however, already married to a beautiful Roman lady named Junia Silana. Silana had been, and was still at this time, an intimate friend of Agrippina, Nero's mother;
though in subsequent times they became bitter enemies. Messalina made no secret of
her love for Silius. She visited him freely at
his house, and received his visits in return;
she accompanied him to public places, evincing everywhere her strong regard for him in

the most undisguised and open manner. At
length she proposed to him to divorce his wife,
in order that she herself might enjoy his society without any limitation or restraint. Silius
hesitated for a time about complying with
these proposals. He was well aware that he
must necessarily incur great danger, either by
complying or by refusing to comply with
them.   To accede to the empress's proposals,
would be of course to place himself in a position of extreme peril; and the fate of Silanus
was a warning to him of what he had to fear
from her wrath, in case of a refusal.   He
concluded that the former danger was on the
whole the least to be apprehended, and he
accordingly divorced his wife, and gave himself up wholly to Messalina's will.

This arrangement being made, all things
for a time went on smoothly and well.   Claudius himself lived a very secluded life, and
paid very little attention to his wife's pursuits
or pleasures. He lived sometimes in retirement
in his palace, devoting his time to his studies,
or to the plans and measures of government.
He seems to have honestly desired to promote
the welfare and prosperity of the republic,
and he made many useful regulations and

74   NERO.   [A.D. 47

Public works at Ostia.   The obelisk.   Immense ship.

laws which promised to be conducive to this
end. Sometimes he was absent for a season
from the city,—visiting fortresses and encampments, or inspecting the public works,
such as aqueducts and canals, which were in
progress of construction. He was particularly
interested in certain operations which he
planned and conducted at the mouths of the
Tiber for forming a harbor there. The place
was called Ostia, that word in the Latin
tongue denoting *mouths*. To form a port
there he built two long piers, extending them
in a curvilinear form into the sea, so as to in-
close a large area of water between them,
where ships could lie at anchor in safety.
Light-houses were built at the extremities of
these piers. It is a curious circumstance that
in forming the foundation of one of these
piers, the engineers whom Claudius employed
sunk an immense ship which Caligula had
formerly caused to be built for the purpose of
transporting an obelisk from Egypt to Rome,
—the obelisk which now stands in front of
St. Peter's Church, and is the admiration and
wonder of all visitors to Rome. As the obelisk
was formed of a single stone, a vessel of a very
large size and of an unusual construction was

necessary for the conveyance of it; and when this ship had once delivered its monstrous burden, it had no longer any useful function to perform on the surface of the sea, and the engineers accordingly filled it with stones and gravel, and sunk it at the mouth of the Tiber, to form part of the foundation of one of Claudius's piers.   As it is found that there is no perceptible decay, even for centuries, in timber that is kept constantly submerged in the water of the sea, it is not impossible that the vast hulk, unless marine insects have devoured it and carried it away, lies imbedded where Claudius placed it, still.

While the emperor was engaged in these and similar pursuits and occupations, Messalina went on in her career of dissipation and indulgence from bad to worse, growing more and more bold and open every day. She lived in a constant round of entertainments and of gayety—sometimes receiving companies of guests at her own palace, and sometimes making visits with a large retinue of attendants and friends, at the house of Silius. Of course, every one paid court to Silius, and assumed, in their intercourse with him, every appearance that they entertained for him the

most friendly regard. It is always so with
the favorites of the great. While in heart
they are hated and despised, in form and ap
pearance they are caressed and applauded.
Silius was intoxicated with the emotions that
the giddy elevation to which he had arrived
so naturally inspired. He was not, however,
wholly at his ease. He could not but be aware
that lofty as his position was, it was the brink
of a precipice that he stood upon. Still he
shut his eyes in a great measure to his danger
and went blindly on. The catastrophe, which
came very suddenly at last, will form the
subject of the next chapter.

CHAPTER IV.
THE FATE OF MESSALINA.

AS might naturally have been expected, there were two very different emotions awakened in the mind of Silius by the situation in which he found himself placed with Messalina,—one was ambition, and the other was fear. Finding himself suddenly raised to the possession of so high a degree of consideration and influence, it was natural that he should look still higher, and begin to wish for actual and official power. And then, on the other hand, his uneasiness at the dangers that he was exposed to by remaining as he was, increased every day. At length a plan occurred to him which both these considerations urged him to adopt. The plan was to murder Claudius, and then to marry Messalina, and make himself emperor in Claudius's place. By the accomplishment of this design he would effect, he thought, a double object. He would at once raise himself to a post of real and substantial power, and also, at the

same time place himself in a position of se
curity. He resolved to propose this scheme
to Messalina.

Accordingly, on the first favorable oppor
tunity, he addressed the empress on the subject, and cautiously made known his design
"I wish to have you wholly mine," said he,
" and although the emperor is growing old,
we can not safely wait for his death. We are,
in fact, continually exposed to danger. We
have gone quite too far to be safe where we
are, and by taking the remaining steps necessary to accomplish fully our ends we shall
only be completing what we have begun, and
by so doing, far from incurring any new pen-
alties, we shall be taking the only effectual
method to protect ourselves from the dangers
which impend over us and threaten us now
Let us, therefore, devise some means to remove the emperor out of our way. I will
then be proclaimed emperor in his place, and
be married to you. The power which you
now enjoy will then come back to you again,
undiminished, and under such circumstances
as will render it permanently secure to you.
To accomplish this will be very easy; for the
emperor, superannuated, infirm, and stupid

as he is, can not protect himself against any well-planned and vigorous attempt which we may make to remove him; though, if we remain as we are, and any accidental cause should arouse him from his lethargy, we may expect to find him vindictive and furious against us to the last degree."

Messalina listened to this proposal with great attention and interest, but so far as related to the proposed assassination of the emperor she did not seem inclined to assent to it. Her historian says that she was not influenced in this decision by any remaining sentiments of conjugal affection, or by conscientious principle of any kind, but by her distrust of Silius, and her unwillingness to commit herself so entirely into his power. She preferred to keep him dependent upon her, rather than to make herself dependent upon him. She liked the plan, however, of being married to him, she said, and would consent to that, even while the emperor remained alive. And so if Silius would agree to it, she was ready, she added, the next time that the emperor went to Ostia, to have the ceremony performed.

That a wife and a mother, however unprincipled and corrupt, should make, under such circumstances, a proposal like this of Messalina's, is certainly very extraordinary; and to those who do not know to what extremes of recklessness and infatuation, the irresponsible despots that have arisen from time to time to rule mankind, have often pushed their wickedness and crime, it must seem wholly incredible. The Roman historian who has recorded this narrative, assures us, that it was the very audacity of this guilt that constituted its charm in Messalina's eyes. She had become weary of, and satiated with, all the ordinary forms of criminal indulgence and pleasure. The work of deceiving and imposing upon her husband, in order to secure for herself the gratifications which she sought, was for a time sufficient to give zest and piquancy to her pleasures. But he was so easily deceived, and she had been accustomed to deceive him so long, that it now no longer afforded to her mind any stimulus or excitement to do it in any common way. But the idea of being actually married to another man while he was absent at a short distance from the city, would be something striking and new, which would vary, she thought, the dull monotony of the common course of sin.

The proposed marriage was finally determined upon, and the mock ceremony, for such
a ceremony could, of course, have no legal
force, was duly performed at a time when
Claudius was absent at Ostia, inspecting the
works which were in progress there. How far
the pretended marriage was open and public
in the actual celebration of it, is not very certain; but the historians say that it was conducted with all the usual ceremonies, and
was attended by the usual witnesses. The
service was performed by the *augur*, a sort
of sacerdotal officer, on whom the duty of
conducting such solemnities properly devolved. Messalina and Silius, each in their
turn, repeated the words pertaining respec-
tively to the bridegroom and the bride. The
usual sacrifice to the gods was then made,
and a nuptial banquet followed, at which
there passed between the new married pair
the caresses and endearments usual on such
occasions. All things in a word were conducted, from the beginning to the end, as in
a real and honest wedding, and whether the
scene thus enacted was performed in public
as a serious transaction, or at some private
entertainment as a species of sport, it created

15—6

a strong sensation among all who witnessed it, and the news of it soon spread abroad and became very generally known.

The more immediate friends of Claudius were very indignant at such a proceeding. They conferred together, uttering to each other many murmurings and complaints, and anticipating the worst results and consequences from what had occurred. Silius, they said, was an ambitious and dangerous man, and the audacious deed which he had performed was the prelude, they believed, to some deep ulterior design. They feared for the safety of Claudius ; and as they knew very well that the downfall of the emperor would involve them too in ruin, they were naturally much alarmed. It was, however, very diffi cult for them to decide what to do.

If they were to inform the emperor of Mes salina's proceedings, they considered it wholly uncertain what effect the communication would have upon him. Like almost all weak-minded men, he was impulsive and capricious in the extreme ; and whether, on a communication being made to him, he would receive it with indifference and unconcern, or, in case his anger should be aroused, whether it would expend itself upon Messalina or upon those who informed him against her, it was wholly impossible to foresee.

At length, after various consultations and debates, a small number of the courtiers who were most determined in their detestation of Messalina and her practices, leagued themselves together, and resolved upon a course of procedure by which they hoped, if possible, to effect her destruction. The leader of this company was Callistus, one of the officers of Claudius's household. He was one of the men who had been engaged with Chærea in the assassination of Caligula. Narcissus was another. This was the same Narcissus that is mentioned in the last chapter, as the artful contriver, with Messalina, of the death of Silanus. Pallas was the name of a third conspirator. He was a confidential friend and favorite of Claudius, and was very jealous, like the rest, of the influence which Silius, through Messalina, exercised over his master. These were the principal confederates, though there were some others joined with them.

The great object of the hostility of these men, seems to have been Silius, rather than Messalina. This, in fact, would naturally be

supposed to be the case, since it was Silius
rather than Messalina who was their rival.
Some of them appear to have hated Messalina
on her own account, but with the others there
was apparently no wish to harm the empress,
if any other way could be found of reaching
Silius. In fact, in the consultations which
were held, one plan which was proposed was
to go to Messalina, and without evincing any
feelings of unkindness or hostility toward her,
to endeavor to persuade her to break off her
connection with her favorite. This plan was,
however, soon overruled. The plotters thought
that it would be extremely improbable that
Messalina would listen to any such proposition,
and in case of her rejection of it, if it were
made, her anger would be aroused strongly
against them for making it: and then, even
if she should not attempt to take vengeance
upon them for their presumption, she would
at any rate put herself effectually upon her
guard against any thing else which they
should attempt to do. The plan of separating
Messalina and Silius was, therefore, abandoned, and the determination resolved upon to
take measures for destroying them both together.

The course which the confederates decided
to pursue in order to effect their object, was
to proceed to Ostia, where Claudius still remained, and there make known to him what
Messalina and Silius had done, and endeavor
to convince him that this audacious conduct
on their part was only the prelude to open
violence against the life of the emperor. It
would seem, however, that no one of them
was quite willing to take upon himself the office of making such a communication as this,
in the first instance, to such a man. They did
not know how he would receive it,—or against
whom the first weight of his resentment and
rage would fall. Finally, after much hesitation and debate, they concluded to employ a
certain female for the purpose,—a courtesan
named Calpurnia. Calpurnia was a favorite
and companion of Claudius, and as such they
thought she might perhaps have an opportunity to approach him with the subject under
such circumstances as to diminish the danger.
At any rate, Calpurnia was easily led by such
inducements as the conspirators laid before
her, to undertake the commission. They not
only promised her suitable rewards, but they
appealed also to the jealousy and hatred which

6

such a woman would naturally feel toward
Messalina, who, being a wife, while Calpurnia
was only a companion and favorite, would
of course be regarded as a rival and enemy
They represented to Calpurnia how entirely
changed for the better her situation would be,
if Messalina could once be put out of the way.
There would then, they said, be none to interfere with her ; but her influence and ascendency over the emperor's mind would be established on a permanent and lasting footing.

Calpurnia was very easily led by these inducements to undertake the commission.
There was another courtesan named Cleopatra, who, it was arranged, should be at hand
when Calpurnia made her communication,
to confirm the truth of it, should any confirmation seem to be required. The other conspirators, also, were to be near, ready to be
called in and to act as occasion might require,
in case Calpurnia and Cleopatra should find
that their statement was making the right impression. Things being all thus arranged the
party proceeded to Ostia to carry their plans
into execution.

In the mean time Messalina and Silius,
wholly unconscious of the danger, gave them

selves up with greater and greater boldness and unconcern to their guilty pleasures. On the day when Callistus and his party went to Ostia she was celebrating a festival at her palace with great gayety and splendor. It was in the autumn of the year, and the festival was in honor of the season. In the countries on the Mediterranean the gathering of grapes and the pressing of the juice for wine, is the great subject of autumnal rejoicings; and Messalina had arranged a festival in accordance with the usual customs, in the gardens of the palace. A wine-press had been erected, and grapes were gathered and brought to it. The guests whom Messalina had invited were assembled around; some were dancing about the wine-press, some were walking in the alleys, and some were seated in the neighboring bowers. They were dressed in fancy costumes, and their heads were adorned with garlands of flowers. There was a group of dancing girls who were engaged as performers on the occasion, to dance for the amusement of the company, in honor of Bacchus, the god of wine. These girls were dressed, so far as they were clothed at all, in robes made of the skins of tigers, and their

heads were crowned with flowers. Messalina
herself, however, was the most conspicuous
object among the gay throng. She was robed
in a manner to display most fully the graces
of her person; her long hair waving loosely
in the wind. She had in her hand a symbol,
or badge, called the *thyrsus*, which was an
ornamented staff, or pole, surmounted with a
carved representation of a bunch of grapes,
and with other ornaments and emblems. The
thyrsus was always used in the rites and festivities celebrated in honor of Bacchus. Silius
himself, dressed like the rest in a fantastic
and theatrical costume, danced by the side of
Messalina, in the center of a ring of dancing
girls which was formed around them.

In the mean time, while this gay party
were thus enjoying themselves in the palace
gardens at Rome, a very different scene was
enacting at Ostia. Calpurnia, in her secret
interview with Claudius, seizing upon a moment which seemed to her favorable for her
purpose, kneeled down before him and made
the communication with which she had been
charged. She told him of Messalina's conduct, and informed him particularly how she
had at last crowned the dishonor of her hus-

MESSALINA IN THE GARDEN.

LONDON:—BRADBURY.

band by openly marrying Silius, or at least pretending to do so. "Your friends believe," she added, "that she and Silius entertain still more criminal designs, and that your life will be sacrificed unless you immediately adopt vigorous and decided measures to avert the danger."

Claudius was very much amazed, and was also exceedingly terrified at this communication. He trembled and turned pale, then looked wild and excited, and began to make inquiries in an incoherent and distracted manner. Calpurnia called in Cleopatra to confirm her story. Cleopatra did confirm it, of course, in the fullest and most unqualified manner. The effect which was produced upon the mind of the emperor seemed to be exactly what the conspirators had desired. He evinced no disposition to justify or to defend Messalina, or to be angry with Calpurnia and Cleopatra for making such charges against her. His mind seemed to be wholly absorbed with a sense of the dangers of his situation, and Narcissus was accordingly sent for to come in.

Narcissus, when appealed to, acknowledged, though with well-feigned reluctance and hesitation, the truth of what Calpurnia had de-

clared, and he immediately began to apolo-
gize for his own remissness in not having
before made the case known.   He spoke with
great moderation of Messalina, and also of
Silius, as if his object were to appease rather
than to inflame the anger of the emperor.
He however admitted, he said, that it was
absolutely necessary that something decisive
should be done.   " Your wife is taken from
you," said he, "and Silius is master of her.
The next thing will be that he will be master
of the republic.   He may even already have
gained the Prætorian guards over to his side,
in which case all is lost.   It is absolutely necessary that some immediate and decisive action should be taken."

Claudius, in great trepidation, immediately
called together such of his prominent councillors and friends as were at hand at Ostia, to
consult on what was to be done.   Of course,
it was principally the conspirators themselves
that appeared at this council.   They crowded
around the emperor and urged him immediately to take the most decisive measures to
save himself from the impending danger, and
they succeeded so well in working upon his
fears that he stood before them in stupid

amazement, wholly incapable of deciding what to say or do. The conspirators urged upon the emperor the necessity of first securing the guard. This body was commanded by an officer named Geta, on whom Narcissus said no reliance could be placed, and he begged that Claudius would immediately authorize him, Narcissus, to take the command. The object of the confederates in thus wishing to get command of the guard was, perhaps, to make sure of the prompt and immediate exe cution of any sentence which they might suc ceed in inducing the emperor to pronounce upon Silius or Messalina, before he should have the opportunity of changing his mind. The emperor turned from one adviser to an other, listening to their various suggestions and plans, but he seemed bewildered and un decided, as if he knew not what to do. It was, however, at length, determined to proceed immediately to Rome The whole party accordingly mounted into their carriages, Narcissus taking his seat by the side of the emperor in the imperial chariot, in order that he might keep up the excitement and agitation in his master's mind by his conversation on the way.

In the mean time there were among those
who witnessed these proceedings at Ostia,
some who were disposed to take sides with
Messalina and Silius, in the approaching
struggle; and they immediately dispatched a
special messenger to Rome to warn the empress of the impending danger. This messenger rode up along the banks of the Tiber with
all speed, and in advance of the emperor's
party. On his arrival in the city he immediately repaired to the palace gardens and communicated his errand to Messalina and her
company in the midst of their festivities.
Claudius had been informed, he said, against
her and Silius, and was almost beside himself with resentment and anger. He was already on his way to Rome, the messenger
added, coming to wreak vengeance upon
them, and he warned them to escape for their
lives. This communication was made, of
course, in the first instance, somewhat privately to the parties principally concerned.
It, however, put a sudden stop to all the hilar-
ity and joy, and the tidings were rapidly circulated around the gardens. One man
climbed into a tree and looked off in the direction of Ostia. The others asked him what

he saw. "I see a great storm arising from the sea at Ostia," said he, "and coming hither, and it is time for us to save ourselves." In a word the bacchanalian games and sports were all soon broken up in confusion, and the company made their escape from the scene, each by a different way.

Silius immediately resumed his ordinary dress, and went forth into the city, where, under an assumed appearance of indifference and unconcern, he walked about in the forum, as if nothing unusual had occurred. Messalina herself fled to the house of a friend, named Lucullus, and, passing immediately through the house, sought a hiding-place in the gardens. Here her mind began to be overwhelmed with anguish, remorse, and terror. Her sins, now that a terrible retribution for them seemed to be impending, rose before her in all their enormity, and she knew not what to do. She soon reflected that there could be no permanent safety for her where she was, for the advanced guards of Claudius, which were even then entering the city and commencing their arrests, would be sure soon to discover the place of her retreat, and bring her before her exasperated husband. She concluded that, rather than wait for this, it would be better for her to go before him herself voluntarily; and, by throwing herself upon his mercy, endeavor to soften and appease him. She accordingly, in her distraction, determined to pursue this course. She came forth from her hiding-place in Lucullus's gardens, and went to seek her children, intending to take them with her, that the sight of them might help to move the heart of their father. Her children were two in number. Octavia, who has already been mentioned, was the eldest, being now about ten or twelve years of age. The other was a boy several years younger; his name was Britannicus.

In the mean time, the city was thrown quite into a state of commotion, by the approach of Claudius, and by the tidings which had spread rapidly through the streets, of what had occurred. The soldiers whom Claudius had sent forward, were making arrests in the streets, and searching the houses. In the midst of this excitement, Messalina, with her children, attended by one of the vestal virgins, named Vibidia, whom she had prevailed upon to accompany her and plead her cause, came forth from her palace on foot, and proceeded through the streets, her hair disheveled, her dress in disorder, and her whole appearance marked by every characteristic of humiliation, abasement, and woe. When she reached the gate of the city, she mounted into a common cart which she found there, and in that manner proceeded to meet her angry husband, leaving her children with Vibidia, the vestal, to follow behind.

She had not proceeded very far, before she met the emperor's train approaching. As soon as she came near enough to the carriage of Claudius to be heard, she began to utter loud entreaties and lamentations, begging her husband to hear before he condemned her. "Hear your unhappy wife," said she, "hear the mother of Britannicus and Octavia." Narcissus and the others who were near, interposed to prevent her from being heard. They talked continually to the emperor, and produced a written memorial and other papers for him to read, which contained, they said, a full account of the whole transaction. Claudius, taking very little notice of his wife, pursued his way toward the city. She followed in his train. When they drew near to the gates, they met Vibidia and the children

15—7

Vibidia attempted to speak, but Claudius would not listen. She complained, in a mournful tone, that for him to condemn his wife unheard, would be unjust and cruel; but Claudius was unmoved. He told Vibidia that Messalina would in due time have a suitable opportunity to make her defense, and that, in the mean time, the proper duty of a vestal virgin was to confine herself to the functions of her sacred office. Thus he sent both her and the children away.

As soon as the party arrived in the city Narcissus conducted the emperor to the house of Silius, and entering it he showed to the emperor there a great number of proofs of the guilty favoritism which the owner of it had enjoyed with Messalina. The house was filled with valuable presents, the tokens of Messalaina's love, consisting, many of them, of costly household treasures which had descended to Claudius in the imperial line, and which were of such a character that the alienation of them by Messalina, in such a way, was calculated to fill the heart of Claudius with indignation and anger. The emperor then proceeded to the camp. Silius and several of his leading friends were arrested and brought together before a sort of military tribunal summoned on the spot to try them. The trial was of course very brief and very summary. They were all condemned to death and were led out to instant execution.

This being done the emperor returned with his friends to the city and repaired to his palace. His mind seemed greatly relieved. He felt that the crisis of danger was past. He ordered supper to be prepared, and when it was ready he seated himself at table. He congratulated himself and his friends on the escape from the perils that had surrounded them, which they had so happily accomplished. Narcissus and the others began to tremble lest after all Messalina should be spared; and they knew full well that if she should be allowed to live, she would soon, by her artful management, regain her ascendency over the emperor's mind, and that in that case she would give herself no rest until she had destroyed all those who had taken any part in effecting the destruction of Silius. They began to be greatly alarmed therefore for their own safety. In the mean time messages came in from Messalina, who, when the emperor entered the city, had returned to her

100   N E R O.   [A.D. 48

Messalina's letter.   Claudius relents.   Alarm of Narcissus.

former place of refuge in the gardens of Lucullus.   At length a letter, or memorial,
came. On reading what was written it was
found that Messalina was assuming a bolder
tone. Her letter was a remonstrance rather
than a petition, as if she were designing to try
the effect of bravery and assurance, and to
see if she could not openly reassume the ascendency and control which she had long exercised over the mind of her husband.   Claudius seemed inclined to hesitate and waver.
His anger appeared to be subsiding with his
fears, and the wine which he drank freely at
the table seemed to conspire with the other
influences of the occasion to restore his wonted
good-humor.   He ordered that in reply to
Messalina's letter a messenger should go and
inform her that she should be admitted the
next day to see him and to make her defense.

Narcissus and his confederates were greatly
alarmed, and determined immediately that
this must not be. Narcissus had been placed,
t would seem, according to the wish of the
conspirators at the outset, in command of the
guard; and he accordingly had power to prevent the emperor's determination from being
carried into effect, provided that he should

dare to take the responsibility of acting. It was a moment of great anxiety and suspense He soon, however, came strongly to the conclusion that though it would be very dangerous for him to act, yet that not to act would be certain destruction; since if Messalina were allowed to live it would be absolutely certain that they all must die. Accordingly, summoning all his resolution he hurried out of the banqueting room, and gave orders to the officers on duty there, in the emperor's name, to proceed to the gardens of Lucullus and execute sentence of death on Messalina without any delay.

Messalina was with her mother Lepida, in the gardens, awaiting her answer from the emperor, when the band of soldiers came Messalina and her mother had never been agreed, and now for a long time had had no intercourse with each other. The daughter's danger had, however, reawakened the instinct of maternal love in the mother's heart, and Lepida had come to see her child in this the hour of her extremity. She came, however, not to console or comfort her child, or to aid her in her efforts to save her life, but to provide her with the means of putting an end to

7

her own existence as the only way now left to her, of escape from the greater disgrace of public execution.

She accordingly offered a poniard to Messalina in the gardens, and urged her to take it. "Death by your own hand," said she, "is now your only refuge. You *must* die; it is impossible that this tragedy can have any other termination; and to wait quietly here for the stroke of the executioner is base and ignoble. You *must die;*—and all that now remains to you is the power to close the scene with dignity and with becoming spirit."

Messalina manifested the greatest agitation and distress, but she could not summon resolution to receive the poniard. In the midst of this scene the band of soldiers appeared, entering the garden. The mother pressed the poniard upon her daughter, saying, "Now is the time." Messalina took the weapon, and pointed it toward her breast, but had not firmness enough to strike it home. The officer approached her at the head of his men, with his sword drawn in his hand. Messalina, still irresolute, made a feeble and ineffectual effort to give herself a wound, but failed of inflicting it; and then the officer, who had by this time advanced to the spot where she was standing, put an end to her dreadful mental struggles by cutting her down and killing her at a single blow.

When tidings were brought back to Narcissus that his commands had been obeyed, he went again to the presence of Claudius, and reported to him simply that Messalina was no more. He made no explanations, and the emperor asked for none; but went on with his supper as if nothing had occurred, and never afterward expressed any curiosity or interest in respect to Messalina's fate.

As soon as the excitement produced by these transactions had in some degree subsided, various plans and intrigues were commenced for providing the emperor with another wife. There were many competitors for the station, all of whom were eager to occupy it; for, though Claudius was old, imbecile, and ugly, still he was the emperor; and all those ladies of his court who thought that they had any prospect of success, aspired to the possession of his hand, as the summit of earthly ambition. Among the rest, Agrippina appeared. She was Claudius's niece. This relationship was in one respect a bar to her success, since the laws prohibited marriage within that degree of consanguinity. In another respect, however, the relationship was greatly in Agrippina's favor, for under the plea of it she had constant access to the emperor, and was extremely assiduous in her attentions to him. She succeeded, at length, in inspiring him with some sentiment of love, and he determined to make her his wife. The Senate were easily induced to alter the laws in order to enable him to do this, and Claudius and Agrippina were married.

Claudius not only thus made the mother of our hero his wife, but he adopted her son as his son and heir—changing, at the same time, the name of the boy. In place of his former plebeian appellation of Ahenobarbus, he gave him now the imposing title of Nero Claudius Cæsar Drusus Germanicus. He has since generally been known in history, however, by the simple prenomen, Nero.

A.D. 39.] CHILDHOOD OF NERO. 105

Early history of Nero.   Character of his father.

CHAPTER V.

THE CHILDHOOD OF NERO.

DURING the time that Agrippina had been passing through the strange and eventful vicissitudes of her history, described in the preceding chapters, young Nero himself, as we shall henceforth call him, had been growing up an active and intelligent, but an indulged and ungoverned boy. His own father died when he was about three years old. This, however, was an advantage probably, rather than a loss to the boy, as Brazenbeard was an extremely coarse, cruel, and unprincipled man. He once killed one of his slaves for not drinking as much as he ordered him. Riding one day in his chariot through a village, he drove wantonly and purposely over a boy, and killed him on the spot. He defrauded all who dealt with him, and was repeatedly prosecuted for the worst of crimes. He treated his wife with great brutality. As has already been said, he received the announcement of the birth of his

son with derision, saying that nothing but
what was detestable could come from him and
Agrippina; and when they asked him what
name they should give the child, he recommended to them to name him Claudius. This
was said in contempt, for Claudius was at that
time despised by every one, as a deformed
and stupid idiot, though he was subsequently
made emperor in the manner that has been
already explained. The manifestation of such
a spirit, at such a time, on the part of her
husband, pained Agrippina exceedingly,—
but the more it pained her, the more Brazenbeard was gratified and amused. The death
of such a father could, of course, be no calamity.

When Agrippina, Nero's mother, was ban
ished from Rome by the order of Caligula,
Nero himself did not accompany her, but remained behind under the care of his aunt
Lepida, with whom he lived for a time in
comparative neglect and obscurity. Though
he belonged to one of the most aristocratic
families of Rome, his mother being a descendant and heir of the Cæsars, he spent some
years in a situation of poverty and disgrace.
His education was neglected, as he received

no instruction at this time except from a
dancing-master and a barber, who were his
only tutors. Of course, the formation of his
moral character was wholly neglected,—nor,
in fact, considering the character of those by
whom he was surrounded, would it have been
possible that any favorable influence should
have been exerted upon him, if the attempt
had been made.

At length when Caligula died and Agrippina was recalled from her banishment by
Claudius, and reinstated in her former position
at Rome, Nero emerged from his obscurity,
and thenceforth lived with his mother in luxury and splendor in the capital. Nero was a
handsome boy, and he soon became an object
of great popular favor and regard. He often
appeared in public at entertainments and
celebrations, and when he did so he was
always specially noticed and caressed. His
companion, and in some respects his rival and
competitor, at such times, was Britannicus,
the son of Claudius and Messalina. Britan
nicus was two or three years younger than
Nero, and being the son of the emperor was
of course a very prominent and conspicuous
object of attention whenever he appeared.

Bu: the rank of Nero was scarcely less high, since his mother was descended directly from the imperial family, while in age and personal appearance and bearing ne was superior to his cousin.

One instance is specially noticed by the historians of those days, in which young Nero was honored with an extraordinary degree of public attention and regard. It was on the occasion of celebrating what might be called the centennial games. These games were generally supposed to be celebrated at each recurrence of a certain astronomical period, of about one hundred years' duration, called an age; but in reality it was at irregular though very distant intervals that they were observed. Claudius instituted a celebration of them early in his reign. There had been a celebration of them in the reign of Augustus, not many years before,—but Claudius, wishing to sig nalize his own reign by some great entertain ment and display, pretended that Augustus had made a miscalculation, and had observed the festival at the wrong time; and he ordain ed, accordingly, that the celebration should take place again.

The games and shows connected with this

festival extended through three successive
days. They consisted of sacrifices and other
religious rites, dramatic spectacles, athletic
games, and military and gladiatorial shows.
In the course of these diversions there was
celebrated on one of the days what was called
the Trojan game, in which young boys of leading and distinguished families appeared on
horseback in a circus or ring, where they performed certain evolutions and feats of horse-
manship, and mock conflicts, in the midst of
the tens of thousands of spectators who throng-
ed the seats around. Of course Britannicus
and Nero were the most prominent and conspicuous of the boys on this occasion. Nero,
however, in the estimation of the populace,
bore off the palm. He was received with the
loudest acclamations by the whole assembly,
while Britannicus attracted far less attention.
This triumph filled Agrippina's heart with
pride and pleasure, while it occasioned to
Messalina the greatest vexation and chagrin.
It made Agrippina more than ever before the
object of Messalina's hatred and hostility, and
the empress would very probably before long
nave found some means of destroying her
rival had she not soon after this become in-

volved herself in the difficulties arising out of her connection with Silius, which resulted so soon in her own destruction.

The people, however, were filled with admiration of Nero, and they applauded his performance with the utmost enthusiasm. He was for a time a subject of conversation in every circle throughout the city, and many tales were told of his history and his doings. Among other things which were related of him, the story was circulated that Messalina became so excited against him in her jealousy and envy, that she sent two assassins to murder him in his sleep; and that the assassins, coming to him in a garden where he was lying asleep upon a pillow, were just putting their cruel orders into execution when they were driven away by a serpent that appeared miraculously at the moment to defend the child—darting out at the assassins from beneath the pillow. Others said that it was in his infancy that this occurrence took place, and that there were two serpents instead of one, and that they guarded the life of their charge lying with him in his cradle. One of the historians of the time states that neither of these stories was really true, but that they both originated in the fact that Nero was accustomed to wear, when a boy, a bracelet made of a serpent's skin, small and of beautiful colors,—and fastened, as they said, around the wearer's wrist with a clasp of gold.

However the fact may be in respect to Messalina's allowing her jealousy of Agrippina to carry her so far as to make direct attempts upon his life, there is no doubt that she lived in continual fear of the influence both of Nero and of his mother, on the mind of the emperor; and Agrippina was consequently compelled to submit to many indignities which the position and the power of Messalina enabled her to impose upon her enemies and rivals. At length, however, the fall of Messalina, and the entire revolution in the situation and prospects of Agrippina which was consequent upon it, changed altogether the position of Nero. It might have been expected, it is true, even after the marriage of Claudius with Agrippina, that Britannicus would have still maintained altogether the highest place in the emperor's regard, since Britannicus was his own son, while Nero was only the son of his wife. But Agrippina was artful enough to manage her indolent and stupid husband

just as she pleased; and she soon found
means to displace Britannicus, and to raise
Nero in his stead, to the highest place, in
precedence and honor. She persuaded Claudius to adopt Nero as his own son, as was
stated in the last chapter. She obtained a
decree of the Senate, approving and confirm-
ing this act. She then removed Britannicus
from the court and shut him up in seclusion,
in a nursery, under pretense of tender regard
for his health and safety. In a word, she
treated Britannicus in all respects like a little
child, and kept him wholly in the back-
ground; while she brought her own son,
though he was but little older than the other,
very prominently forward, as a young man.

In those ancient days as now, there was
an appropriate dress for youth, which was
changed for that of a man when the subject
arrived at maturity. The garment which was
most distinctively characteristic of adult age
among the Romans was called the toga; and
it was assumed by the Roman youth, not as
the dress of a man is by young persons now,
in a private and informal manner, according
as the convenience or fancy of the individual
may dictate,—but publicly and with much

ceremony, and always at the time when the party arrived at the period of legal majority; so that assuming the toga marked always a very important era of life. This distinction Agrippina caused to be conferred upon Nero by a special edict when he was only fourteen years of age, which was at a very much earlier period than usual. On the occasion of thus advancing him to the dress and to the legal capabilities of manhood, Agrippina brought him out in a special manner before the people of Rome at a great public celebration, and the more effectually to call public attention to him as a young prince of the highest distinction in the imperial family, she induced Claudius to bestow a largess upon the people, and a donative upon the army, that is a public distribution of money, to the citizens and to the soldiers, in Nero's name.

All this time Britannicus was kept shut up in the private apartments of the palace with nurses and children. The tutors and attendants whom Messalina his mother provided for him were one by one removed, and their places supplied by others whom Agrippina selected for the purpose, and whom she could rely upon to second her views. When in

15—8

quired of in respect to Britannicus by those who had known him before, during his mother's lifetime, she replied that he was a weak and feeble child, subject to fits, and thus necessarily kept secluded from society.

Sometimes, indeed, on great public occasions, both Nero and Britannicus appeared together, but even in these cases the arrangements were so made as to impress the public mind more forcibly than ever with an idea of the vast superiority of Nero, in respect to rank and position. On one such occasion, while Britannicus was carried about clothed in the dress of a child, and with attendants characteristic of the nursery, Nero rode on horseback, richly appareled in the triumphal robes of a general returning from a foreign campaign.

Agrippina was one day made very angry with Britannicus, for what might seem a very trifling cause. It seems that Britannicus, though young, was a very intelligent boy, and that he understood perfectly the policy which his step-mother was pursuing toward him, and was very unwilling to submit to be thus supplanted. One day, when he and Nero were both abroad, attending some pub-

lic spectacle or celebration, they met, and
Nero accosted his cousin, calling him Britannicus. Britannicus, in returning the saluta-
tion, addressed Nero familiarly by the name Domitius;—Domitius Ahenobarbus having been
his name before he was adopted by Claudius.
Agrippina was very indignant when she heard
of this. She considered the using of this
name by Britannicus, as denoting, on his
part, a refusal to acknowledge his cousin as
the adopted son of his father. She immediately went to Claudius with earnest and
angry complainings. "Your own edict," said
she, "sanctioned and confirmed by the Sen
ate, is disavowed and annulled, and my son
is subjected to public insult by the imperti
nence of this child." Agrippina farther represented to Claudius, that Britannicus never
would have thought of addressing her son in
such a manner, of his own accord. His doing
it must have arisen from the influence of
some of the persons around him who were
hostile to her; and she made use of the occasion to induce Claudius to give her authority
to remove all that remained of the child's
instructors and governors, who could be suspected of a friendly interest in his cause, and

116   N E R O.   [A.D. 51

The Fucine lake.   Plan for draining it.   The canal.

to subject him to new and more rigorous
restrictions than ever.

One of the most imposing of all the spectacles and celebrations which Claudius instituted during his reign, was the one which
signalized the opening of the canal by which
the Fucine lake was drained. The Fucine
lake was a large but shallow body of water,
at the foot of the Appenines, near the sources
of the Tiber.* It was subject to periodic in-
undations, by which the surrounding lands
were submerged. An engineer had offered
to drain the lake, in consideration of receiving for his pay the lands which would be laid
dry by the operation. But Claudius, who
seemed to have quite a taste for such under-
takings, preferred to accomplish the work
himself. The canal by which the water
should be conveyed away, was to be formed
in part by a deep cut, and partly by a tunnel
through a mountain; and inasmuch as in
those days the power now chiefly relied upon
for making such excavations, namely, the ex-
plosive force of gunpowder, was not known,
any extensive working in solid rock was an
operation of immense labor. When the canal

* See Map. Frontispiece.

was finished, Claudius determined to institute a grand celebration to signalize the opening of it for drawing off the water; and as he could not safely rely on the hydraulic interest of the spectacle for drawing such a concourse to the spot as he wished to see there, he concluded to add to the entertainment a show more suited to the taste and habits of the times. He made arrangements accordingly for having a naval battle fought upon the lake, for the amusement of the spectators, just before the opening of the canal, which was to draw off the water. Thus the battle was to be the closing scene, in which the history and existence of the lake were to be terminated forever.

Ships were accordingly built, and an immense number of men were designated and set apart for fighting the battle. These men consisted of convicts and prisoners of war—men whom it was, in those days, considered perfectly just and right to employ in killing one another for the amusement of the emperor and his guests. A sort of bulwark was built all around the shore, and the emperor's guards were stationed upon it, to prevent the escape of the combatants, and to turn them

8

back to their duty if any of them should attempt, when pressed hard in the battle, to escape to the land. The fleet of galleys was divided into two antagonistic portions, and the men in each were armed completely, as in a case of actual war. At the appointed time, hundreds of thousands of people assembled from all the surrounding country to see the sight. They lined the shores on every side, and crowned all the neighboring heights. The contest, of course, might be waged with all the fury and fatal effect of a real battle without endangering the spectators at all, as there were in those days no flying bullets, or other swift-winged missiles, like those which in modern times take so wide a range beyond the limits of the battle. The deadly effect of all that was done in an ancient combat was confined of course to those immediately engaged. Then there was, besides, nothing to intercept the vision. No smoke was raised to obscure the view, but the atmosphere above and around the combatants remained as pure and transparent at the end of the combat as at the beginning.

A real battle was accordingly regarded by the Romans as the most sublime and imposing

A.D. 52.] CHILDHOOD OF NERO. 119

End of the naval battle.   The water will not flow.

of spectacles, and hundreds of thousands of spectators flocked to witness the one which Claudius arranged for them on the Fucine lake. He himself presided, dressed in a coat of mail; and Agrippina sat by his side, clothed in a magnificent robe, which the historian states was woven from threads of gold, without the admixture of any other material. The signal was given, and the battle was commenced. There was some difficulty experienced, as usual in such cases, in getting the men to engage, but they became sufficiently ferocious at last to satisfy all the spectators, and thousands were slain. At length the emperor gave orders that the battle should cease, and the survivors were informed that their lives were spared.

It was fortunate, on the whole, for Claudius, that he did not rely wholly on the simple drawing off of the water from the lake for the amusement of the immense assemblage that he had convened, for it was found, when, after the close of the battle, the canal was opened, that the water would not run. The engineers had made some mistake in their measurements or their calculations, and had left the bed of the canal in some part of its

course too high, so that the water, when the
sluices were opened, instead of flowing off into
the river to which the canal was intended to
conduct it, remained quietly in the lake as
before.

The assembly dispersed, and the work on
the canal was resumed with a view of making
it deeper. In the course of a year the excavation was completed, and all was made
ready for a new trial. Claudius summoned a
new assembly to witness the operation, and at
this time, instead of a naval conflict, he made
provision for a great combat of gladiators, to
be fought on immense floating platforms
which were built upon the lake near the out-
let which the engineers had made. In the
end, however, the second attempt to make the
water flow, proved more unfortunate than the
first. The channel had been made very deep
and wide, so that the water was inclined to
move, when once put in motion, with the utmost impetuosity and force; and it so happened, that in some way or other, the means
which the engineer had relied upon for con
trolling it were insufficient, and when the
gates were opened every thing suddenly gave
way. The water rushed out in an overwhelm

ing torrent, as in an inundation—and under mined and carried away the platforms and stagings which had been erected for the seats of the spectators. A scene of indescribable tumult and confusion ensued. The emperor and empress, with the guests and spectators, fled precipitously together, and all narrowly escaped being carried down into the canal.

It is by no means difficult to imagine what sort of a character a boy must necessarily form, brought up under such influences and surrounded by such scenes as those which thus prevailed at the court of Claudius. It proved in the end that Nero experienced the full effect of them. He became proud, vain, self-willed, cruel, and accustomed to yield himself without restraint to all those wicked propensities and passions which, under such circumstances, always gain dominion over the human soul.

Besides Britannicus, it will be recollected that Messalina had left another child,—a daughter named Octavia, who was two or three years younger than her brother, and of course about five years younger than Nero. Agrippina did not pursue the same course of

opposition and hostility toward her which she
had adopted in regard to Britannicus. She
determined, at the outset, upon a very different plan. Britannicus was necessarily a rival
and competitor for Nero; and every step in
advance which he should make, could not
operate otherwise than as an impediment and
obstacle to Nero's success. But Octavia, as
Agrippina thought, might be employed to
further and aid her designs, by being betroth
ed, and in due time married, to her son.

The advantages of such a scheme were very
obvious,—so obvious in fact that the design
was formed by Agrippina at the very beginning,—even before her own marriage with
the emperor was fully effected. There was
one serious obstacle in the way, and that was
that Octavia was already betrothed to a very
distinguished young nobleman named Lucius
Silanus. Agrippina, after having, by various
skillful manœuvers, succeeded in enlisting the
public officers who would act as judges in his
case, caused Silanus to be accused of infamous crimes. The historians say that the
evidence which was adduced against him was
of the most trivial character. Still he was
condemned He seems to have understood

the nature and the cause of the hostility which had suddenly developed itself against him, and to have felt at once all the hopelessness of his condition. He killed himself in his despair on the very night of the marriage of Claudius with Agrippina.

The empress found afterward no serious difficulty in accomplishing her design. She obtained the emperor's consent to a betrothal of Nero to Octavia; but as they were yet too young to be married, the ceremony was postponed for a short time. At length in about five years after the marriage of Agrippina herself, Nero and Octavia were married. Nero was at that time about sixteen years of age. His bride of course was only eleven.

124   NERO.   [A.D. 54

Claudius is sick.   Agrippina's joy.   Her schemes

CHAPTER VI.

NERO AN EMPEROR.

ABOUT one year after Nero's marriage to Octavia the emperor Claudius was suddenly taken sick. On learning this, Agrippina was very much excited and very much pleased. If the sickness should result in the emperor's death, her son she thought would immediately succeed him. Every thing had been long since fully arranged for such a result, and all was now ready, she imagined, for the change.

It is true that Nero was still very young, but then he was uncommonly mature both in mind and in person, for one of his years; and the people had been accustomed for some time to look upon him as a man. Among other means which Agrippina had resorted to for giving an appearance of manliness and maturity to the character of her son, she had brought him forward in the Roman Forum as a public advocate, and he had made orations there in several instances, with great success.

He had been well instructed in those studies which were connected with the art of oratory, and as his person and manners were agreeable, and his countenance intelligent and prepossessing, and especially as the confidence which he felt in his powers gave him an air of great self-possession and composure, the impression which he made was very favorable. The people were in fact predisposed to be pleased with and to applaud the efforts of a young orator so illustrious in rank and station—and the ability which he displayed, although he was so young, was such as to justify, unquestionably, in some degree, the honors that they paid him.

Agrippina, therefore, supposing that her son was now far enough advanced in public consideration to make it in some degree certain that he would be the emperor's successor, was ready at any time for her husband to die. His sickness therefore filled her mind with excitement and hope. There was another motive too, besides her ambitious desires for the advancement of her son, that made her desirous that Claudius should not live. She had been now for several months somewhat solicitous and anxious about her own safety.

Her influence over Claudius, which was at first so absolute and supreme, had afterward greatly declined, and within a few months she had begun to fear that she might be losing it entirely. In fact she had some reason for believing that Claudius regarded her with concealed hostility and hate, and was secretly revolving plans for deposing both her and her son from the high ascendency to which they had raised themselves, and for bringing back his own son to his proper prominence, in Nero's place. Agrippina, too, in the midst of her ambitious projects and plans, led a life of secret vice and crime, and feeling guilty and self-condemned, every trivial indication of danger excited her fears. Some one informed her that Claudius one day when speaking of a woman who had been convicted of crime, said that it had always been *his* misfortune to have profligate wives, but that he always brought them in the end to the punishment that they deserved. Agrippina was greatly terrified at this report. She considered it a warning that Claudius was meditating some fatal proceedings in respect to her.

Agrippina observed, too, as she thought,

various indications that Claudius was beginning to repent of having adopted Nero and
thus displaced his own son from the line of
inheritance ; and that he was secretly intending to restore Britannicus to his true position.
He treated the boy with greater and greater
attention every day, and at one time, after
having been conversing with him and express
ing an unusual interest in his health and
welfare, he ended by saying, " Go on improv-
ing, my son, and grow up as fast as you can
to be a man. I shall be able to give a good
account of all that I have done in regard to
you in due time. Trust to me, and you will
find that all will come out right in the end."
At another time he told Britannicus that
pretty soon he should give him the *toga*, and
bring him forward before the people as a
man,—" and then at last," said he, " the
Romans will have a prince that is *genuine*."

Agrippina was not present, it is true, when
these things were said and done, but every
thing was minutely reported to her, and she
was filled with anxiety and alarm. She began to be afraid that unless something should
speedily occur to enable her to realize her
hopes and expectations, they would end in

nothing but bitter and cruel disappointment after all.

Such being the state of things, Agrippina was greatly pleased at the news, when she heard that her husband was sick. She most earnestly hoped that he would die, and immediately began to consider what she could do to insure or to hasten such a result. She thought of poison, and began to debate the question in her mind whether she should dare to administer it. Then if she were to decide to give her husband poison, it was a very serious question what kind of poison she should employ. If she were to administer one that was sudden and violent in its operation, the effect which it would produce might attract attention, and her crime be discovered. On the other hand, if she were to choose one that was more moderate and gradual in its power, so as to produce a slow and lingering death, time would be allowed for Claudius to carry into effect any secret designs that he might be forming for disavowing Nero as his son, and fixing the succession upon Britannicus; and Agrippina well knew that if Claudius were to die, leaving things in such a state that Britannicus should succeed him, the downfall and ruin both of herself and her son would immediately and inevitably follow.

There was at that time in Rome a celebra-ted mistress of the art of poisoning, named Locusta. She was in prison, having been condemned to death for her crimes. Though condemned she had been kept back from execution by the influence of Agrippina, on account of the skill which she possessed in her art, and which Agrippina thought it possible that she might have occasion at some time to make use of. This Locusta she now determined to consult. She accordingly went to her, and asked her if she did not know of any poison which would immediately take effect upon the brain and mind, so as to incapacitate the patient at once from all mental action, while yet it should be gradual and slow in its operations on the vital functions of the body. Locusta answered in the affirmative. Such characters were always prepared to furnish any species of medicaments that their customers might call for. She compounded a potion which she said possessed the properties which Agrippina required, and Agrippina, receiving it from her hands, went away.

Agrippina then went to Halotus, the servant

15—9

who waited upon the emperor and gave him his
food,—and contrived some means to induce him
to administer the dose. Halotus was the emperor's "taster," as it was termed :—that is, it
was his duty to taste first, himself, every ar-
ticle of food or drink which he offered to his
master, for the express purpose of making it
sure that nothing was poisoned. It is obvious,
however, that many ways might be devised
for evading such a precaution as this, and
Halotus and Agrippina arranged it, that the
poison, in this case, should be put upon a dish
of mushrooms, and served to the emperor at
his supper. The taster was to avoid, by
means of some dextrous management, the
taking of any portion of the fatal ingredients
himself. The plan thus arranged was put
into execution. The emperor ate the mushrooms, and Agrippina tremblingly awaited
the result.

She was, however, disappointed in the effect
that was produced. Whether the mixture that
Locusta had prepared was not sufficiently
powerful, or whether Halotus in his extreme
anxiety not to get any of the poisonous ingredients himself failed to administer them effectually to his intended victim, the emperor

seemed to continue afterward much as he had
been before,—still sick, but without any new
or more dangerous symptoms. Of course,
Agrippina was in a state of great solicitude
and apprehension. Having incurred the terrible guilt and danger necessarily involved
in an attempt to poison her husband, she
could not draw back. The work that was
begun must be carried through now, she
thought, at all hazards, to its termination;
and she immediately set herself at work to
devise some means of reaching her victim
with poison, which would avoid the taster altogether, and thus not be liable to any interference on his part, dictated either by his
fidelity to his master or his fears for himself.
She went, accordingly, to the emperor's
physician and found means to enlist him in
her cause; and a plan was formed between
them which proved effectual in accomplishing
her designs. The manner in which they contrived it was this. The physician, at a time
when the emperor was lying sick and in distress upon his couch, came to him and proposed that he should open his mouth and allow the physician to touch his throat with the
tip of a feather, to promote vomiting, which

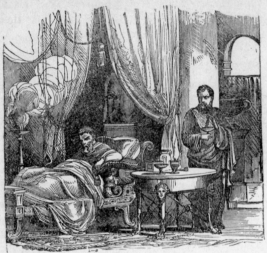

The Poisoning of Claudius.

he said he thought would relieve him. The
emperor yielded to this treatment, and the
feather was applied. It had previously been
dipped in a very virulent and fatal poison.
The poison thus administered took effect, and
Claudius, after passing the night in agony,
died early in the morning.

Of course, Agrippina, when her husband's
dying struggles were over, and she was satisfied that life was extinct, experienced for the

moment a feeling of gratification and relief.
It might have been expected, however, that
the pangs of remorse, after the deed was per
petrated, would have followed very hard upon
the termination of her suspense and anxiety.
But it was not so.   Much still remained to be
done, and Agrippina was fully prepared to
meet all the responsibilities of the crisis. The
death of her husband took place very early in
the morning, the poisoning operations having
been performed in the night, and having accomplished their final effect about the break
of day.   Agrippina immediately perceived
that the most effectual means of accomplishing the end which she had in view, was not
to allow of any interval to elapse between the
announcement of the emperor's death and the
bringing forward of her son for induction into
office as his successor ; since during such an
interval, if one were allowed, the Roman people would, of course, discuss the question,
whether Britannicus or Nero should succeed
o power, and a strong party might possibly
organize itself to enforce the claims of the
former.   She determined, therefore, to con
ceal the death of her husband until noon, the
hour most favorable for publicly proclaiming

9

any great event, and then to announce the death of the father and the accession of the adopted son together.

She accordingly took prompt and decisive measures to prevent its being known that the emperor was dead. The immediate attendants at his bedside could not indeed be easily deceived, but they were required to be silent in respect to what had occurred, and to go on with all their services and ministrations just as if their patient were still alive. Visitors were excluded from the room, and messengers were kept coming to and fro with baths, medicaments, and other appliances, such as a desperate crisis in a sick chamber might be supposed to require. The Senate was convened, too, in the course of the morning, and Agrippina, as if in great distress, sent a message to them, informing them of her husband's dangerous condition, and entreating them to join with the chief civil and religious functionaries of the city, in offering vows, supplications, and sacrifices for his recovery. She herself, in the mean time, went from room to room about the palace, overwhelmed to all appearance, with anxiety and grief. She kept Britannicus and his sisters all the time with her, folding the boy in her arms with an appearance of the fondest affection, and telling him how heart-broken she was at the danger)us condition of his father. She kept Britannicus thus constantly near to her, in order to prevent the possibility of his being seized and carried away to the camp by any party that might be disposed to make him emperor rather than Nero, when it should be known that Claudius had ceased to reign. As an additional defense against this danger, Agrippina brought up a cohort of the life-guards around the palace, and caused them to be stationed in such a manner that every avenue of approach to the edifice was completely secured. The cohort which she selected was one that she thought she could most safely rely upon, not only for guarding the palace while she remained within it, but for proclaiming Nero as emperor when she should at last be ready to come forth and announce the death of her husband.

At length, about noon, she deemed that the hour had arrived, and after placing Britannicus and his sisters in some safe custody within the palace, she ordered the gates to be thrown open, and prepared to come forth to announce the death of Claudius, and to present Nero to the army and to the people of Rome, as his rightful successor. She was aided and supported in these preparations by a number of officers and attendants, among whom were the two whom she had determined upon as the two principal ministers of her son's government. These were Seneca and Burrus. Seneca was to be minister of state, and Burrus the chief military commander.

Both these men had long been in the service of Agrippina and of Nero. Seneca was now over fifty years of age. He was very highly distinguished as a scholar and rhetorician while he lived, and his numerous writings have given him great celebrity since, in every age. He commenced his career in Rome as a public advocate in the Forum, during the reign of Caligula. After Caligula's death he incurred the displeasure of Claudius in the first year of that emperor's reign, and he was banished to the island of Corsica, where he remained in neglect and obscurity for about eight years. When at length Messalina was put to death, and the emperor married Agrippina, Seneca was par doned and recalled through Agrippina's influence, and after that he devoted himself very faithfully to the service of the empress and of her son. Agrippina appointed him Nero's preceptor, and gave him the direction of all the studies which her son pursued in qualifying himself for the duties of a public orator; and now that she was about attempting to advance her son to the supreme command, she intended to make the philosopher his principal secretary and minister of state.

Burrus was the commander of the lifeguards, or as the office was called in those days, prefect of the prætorium. The lifeguards, or body-guards, whose duty consisted exclusively in attending upon, escorting and protecting the emperor, consisted of ten cohorts, each containing about a thousand men. The soldiers designated for this service were of course selected from the whole army, and as no expense was spared in providing them with arms, accoutrements and other appointments, they formed the finest body of troops in the world. They received double pay, and enjoyed special privileges; and every arrangement was made to secure their entire subserviency to the will, and attachment to

the person, of the reigning emperor. Of
course such a corps would be regarded by all
the other divisions of the army as entirely
superior in rank and consideration, to the ordinary service; and the general who commanded them would take precedence of every
other military commander, being second only
to the emperor himself. Agrippina had contrived to raise Burrus to this post through her
influence with Claudius. He was a friend to
her interests before, and he became still more
devoted to her after receiving such an appointment through her instrumentality.—
Agrippina now depended upon Burrus to
carry the Prætorian cohorts in favor of her
son.

Accordingly at noon of the day on which
Claudius died, when all things were ready,
the palace gates were thrown open and Agrippina came forth with her son, accompanied
by Burrus and by other attendants. The cohort on duty was drawn up under arms at the
palace gates. Burrus presented Nero to them
as the successor of Claudius, and at a signal
from him they all responded with shouts and
acclamations. Some few of the soldiers did
not join in this cheering, but looked on in si

lence, and then inquired of one another what had become of Britannicus. But there were none to answer this question, and as no one appeared to proclaim Britannicus or to speak in his name, the whole cohort finally acquiesced in the decision to which the majority, at the instigation of Burrus, seemed inclined. A sort of chair or open palanquin was provided, and Nero was mounted upon it. He was borne in this way by the soldiers through the streets of the city, escorted by the cohort on the way, till he reached the camp. As the procession moved along, the air was filled with the shouts and acclamations of the soldiers and of the people.

When the party arrived at the camp Nero was presented to the army, and the officers and soldiers being drawn up before him he delivered a brief speech which Seneca had prepared for the occasion. The principal point in this speech, and the one on which its effect was expected to depend, was a promise of a large distribution of money. The soldiers always expected such a donative on the accession of any new emperor,—but Nero, in order to suppress any latent opposition which might be felt against his claims, made his proposed dis-

tribution unusually large. The soldiers readily yielded to the influence of this promise,
and with one accord proclaimed Nero emperor. The Senate was soon afterward convened, and partly through the influence of
certain prominent members whom Agrippina
had taken measures to secure in her interest,
and partly through the general conviction that
as things were the claims of Britannicus could
not be successfully maintained, the choice of
the army was confirmed. And as the tidings
of what had taken place at the capital gradu
ally spread through Italy and to the remoter
portions of the empire, the provinces, and the
various legions at their encampments, one
after another acquiesced in the result, both
because on the one hand they had no strong
motive for dissenting, and on the other, they
had individually no power to make any effectual resistance. Thus Nero, at the age of
seventeen became emperor of Rome, and as
such the almost absolute monarch of nearly
half the world.

It was, however, by no means the design
of Agrippina that her son should actually
wield, himself, all this power. Her motive,
in all her manœuvers for bringing Nero to

this lofty position, was a personal, not a maternal ambition. She was herself to reign, not he; and she had brought him forward as the nominal sovereign only, in order that she might herself exercise the power by acting in his name. Her plan was to secure her own ascendency, by so arranging and directing the course of affairs that the young emperor himself should have as little as possible to do with the duties of his office; and that instead of direct action on his part, all the functions of the government should be fulfilled by officers of various grades, whom she was herself to appoint and to sustain, and who, since they would know that they were dependent on Agrippina's influence for their elevation, would naturally be subservient to her will. Nero being so young, she thought that he could easily be led to acquiesce in such management as this, especially if he were indulged in the full enjoyment of the luxuries and pleasures, innocent or otherwise, which his high station would enable him to command, and which are usually so tempting to one of his character and years.

The first of Agrippina's measures was to make arrangement for a most imposing and magnificent funeral, as the testimonial of the deep conjugal affection which she entertained for her husband, and the profound grief with which she was affected by his death! The most extensive preparations were made for this funeral; and the pomp and parade which were displayed in Rome on the day of the ceremony, had never been surpassed, it was said, by any similar spectacle on any former occasion. In the course of the services that were performed, a funeral oration was delivered by Nero to the immense concourse of people that were convened. The oration was written by Seneca. It was a high panegyric upon the virtues and the renown of the deceased, and it represented in the brightest colors, and with great magnificence of diction, his illustrious birth, the high offices to which he had attained, his taste for the liberal arts, and the peace and tranquillity which had prevailed throughout the empire during his reign. To write a panegyric upon such a man as Claudius had been, must surely have proved a somewhat difficult task; but Seneca accomplished it very adroitly, and the people, aided by the solemnity of the occasion, listened with proper gravity, until at length the orator be-

gan to speak of the judgment and the political
wisdom of Claudius, and then the listeners
found that they could preserve their decorum
no longer. The audience looked at each other,
and there was a general laugh. The young
orator, though for the moment somewhat dis-
concerted at this interruption, soon recovered
himself, and went on to the end of his dis-
course.

After these funeral ceremonies had been
performed, the Senate was convened, and
Nero appeared before them to make his in-
augural address. This address also, was of
course prepared for him by Seneca, under directions from Agrippina, who, after revolving
the subject fully in her mind, had determined
what it would be most politic to say. She
knew very well that until the power of her
son became consolidated and settled, it became
him to be modest in his pretensions and claims,
and to profess great deference and respect for
the powers and prerogatives of the Senate.
In the speech, therefore, which Nero delivered
in the senate-chamber, he said that in assuming the imperial dignity, which he had consented to do in obedience to the will of his
father the late emperor, to the general voice

of the army, and the universal suffrages of the
people, he did not intend to usurp the civil
powers of the state, but to leave to the Senate,
and to the various civil functionaries of the
city, their rightful and proper jurisdiction.
He considered himself as merely the commander-in-chief of the armies of the commonwealth, and as such, his duty would be simply
to execute the national will. He promised,
moreover, a great variety of reforms in the
administration, all tending to diminish the
authority of the prince, and to protect the
people from danger of oppression by military
power. In a word, it was his settled purpose,
he said, to restore the government to its pris-
tine simplicity and purity, and to administer
it in strict accordance with the true principles
of the Roman Constitution, as originally established by the founders of the commonwealth. The professions and promises which
Nero thus made to the Senate, or rather which
he recited to them at the dictation of his
mother and of Seneca, gave great satisfaction
to all who heard them. All opposition to the
claims which he advanced, disappeared, and
the heart of Agrippina was filled with glad-

ness and joy at finding that all her plans had
been so fully and successfully realized.

The official authority of Nero being thus
generally acknowledged, Agrippina began
immediately to pursue a system of policy designed to secure the possession of all real
power for herself, leaving only the name and
semblance of it to her son. She appeared in
all public places with him, sharing with him
the pomp, and parade, and insignia of office,
as if she were associated with him in official
power. She received and opened the dispatches and sent answers to them. She considered and decided questions of state, and
issued her orders. She caused several influential persons whom she supposed likely to
take part with Britannicus, or at least secretly
to favor his claims, to be put to death, either
by violence or by poison; and she would have
caused the death of many others in this way,
if Burrus and Seneca had not interposed their
influence to prevent it. She did all these
things in a somewhat covert and cautious
manner, acting generally in Nero's name, so
as not to attract too much attention at first to
her measures. There was danger, she knew,
of awakening resistance and opposition, as

public sentiment among the Romans had
always been entirely averse to the idea of the
ubmission of men, in any form, to the government of women.   Agrippina accordingly did
not attempt openly to preside in the senate-
chamber, but she made arrangements for
having the meetings of the Senate sometimes
held in an apartment of the palace where she
could attend, during the sitting, in an adjoining cabinet, concealed from view by a screen
or arras, and thus listen to the debate.   Even
this, however, was strongly objected to by
some of the senators.   They considered this
arrangement of Agrippina's to be present at
their debates as intended to intimidate them
into the support of such measures as she
might recommend, or be supposed to favor,
and thus as seriously interfering with the
freedom of their discussions. On one occasion
Agrippina made a bolder experiment still, by
coming into the hall where a company of
foreign embassadors were to have audience,
as if it were a part of her official duty to join
in receiving them.   Her son, the emperor,
and the government officers around him, were
confounded when they saw her coming, and
at first did not know what to do. Seneca

however, with great presence of mind, said to Nero, " Your mother is entering, go and receive her." Hereupon, Nero left his chair of state, and accompanied by his ministers, went to meet his mother, and received her with great deference and respect; and the attention of all present was wholly devoted to Agrippina while she remained, as to a very distinguished and highly honored guest,—the business which had called them together being suspended on her account until she withdrew.

Notwithstanding some occasional difficulties and embarrassments of this kind, every thing went on for a time very prosperously, in accordance with Agrippina's wishes and plans. Nero was very young, and little disposed at first to thwart or to resist his mother's measures. He was, however, all the time growing older, and he soon began to grow restive under the domination which Agrippina exercised over him, and to form plans and determinations of his own. There followed, as might have been expected, a terrible conflict for the possession of power between him and his mother. The history and the termination of this struggle will form the subject of the two following chapters.

CHAPTER VII.

BRITANNICUS.

THE occasion which led to the first open outbreak between Agrippina and her son was the discovery on her part of a secret and guilty attachment which had been formed between Nero and a young girl of the palace whose name was Acte. Acte was originally a slave from Asia Minor, having been purchased there and sent to Rome, very probably on account of her personal beauty. She had been subsequently enfranchised, but she remained still in the palace, forming a part of the household of Agrippina. Nero had never felt any strong attachment for Octavia. His marriage he had always regarded as merely one of his mother's political manœuvers, and ne did not consider himself as really bound to his wife by any tie. He was, besides, still but a boy, though unusually precocious and mature; and he had always been accustomed to the most unlimited indulgence of the propensities and passions of youth.

The young prince, as is usual in such cases, was led on and encouraged in the vicious course of life that he was now beginning to pursue, by certain dissolute companions whose society he fell into about this time. There were two young men in particular whose influence over him was of the worst character. Their names were Otho and Senecio. Otho was descended from a very distinguished family, and his rank and social position in Roman society were very high. Senecio, on the other hand, was of a very humble extraction—his father being an emancipated slave. The three young men were, however, nearly of the same age, and being equally unpricipled and dissolute, they banded themselves together in the pursuit and enjoyment of vicious indulgences. Nero made Otho and Senecio his confidants in his connection with Acte and it was in a great measure through thei. assistance and co-operation that he accom plished his ends.

When Seneca and Burrus were informed of Nero's attachment to Acte, and of the connec tion which had been established between them, they were at first much perplexed to know what to do. They were men of strict

10

moral principle themselves, and as Nero had been their pupil, and was still, while they continued his ministers, in some sense under their charge, they thought it might be their duty to remonstrate with him on the course which he was pursuing, and endeavor to separate him from his vicious companions, and bring him back, if possible, to his duty to Octavia. But then, on the other hand, they said to each other that any attempt on their part really to control the ungovernable and lawless propensities of such a soul as Nero's must be utterly unavailing, and since he must necessarily, as they thought, be expected to addict himself to vicious indulgences in some form, the connection with Acte might perhaps be as little to be dreaded as any. On the whole, they concluded not to interfere.

Not so, however, with Agrippina. When she came to learn of this new attachment which her son had formed, she was very much disturbed and alarmed. Her distress, however, did not arise from any of those feelings of solicitude which, as a mother, she might have been expected to feel for the moral purity of her boy, but from fears that, through the influence and ascendency which such a favorite as Acte might acquire, she should lose her own power. She knew very well how absolute and complete the domination of such a favorite sometimes became, and she trembled at the danger which threatened her of being supplanted by Acte, and thus losing her control.

Agrippina was very violent and imperious in her temper, and had long been accustomed to rule those around her with a very high hand; and now, without properly considering that Nero had passed beyond the age in which he could be treated as a mere boy, she attacked him at once with the bitterest reproaches and invectives, and insisted that his connection with Acte should be immediately abandoned. Nero resisted her, and stoutly refused to comply with her demands. Agrippina was fired with indignation and rage. She filled the palace with her complaints and criminations. She accused Nero of the basest ingratitude toward her, in repaying the long-continued and faithful exertions and sacrifices which she had made to promote his interests, by thus displacing her from his confidence and regard, to make room for this wretched favorite, and of false ness and faithlessness to Octavia, in abandoning her, his lawful wife, for the society of an enfranchised slave. Agrippina was extremely violent in these denunciations. She scolded, she stormed, she raved—acting manifestly under the impulse of blind and uncontrollable passion. Her passion was obviously blind, for the course to which it impelled her was plainly very far from tending to accomplish any object which she could be supposed to have in view.

At length, when the first fury of her vexation and anger had spent itself, she began to reflect, as people generally do when recovering from a passion, that she was spending her strength in working mischief to her own cause. This reflection helped to promote the subsiding of her anger. Her loud denunciations gradually died away, and were succeeded by mutterings and murmurings. At length she became silent altogether, and after an interval of reflection, she concluded no longer to give way to her clamorous and useless anger, but calmly to consider what it was best to *do*.

She soon determined that the wisest and most politic plan after all, would be for her to acquiesce in the fancy of her son, and endeavor to retain her ascendency over him by aiding and countenancing him in his pleasures. She accordingly changed by degrees the tone which she had assumed toward him, and began to address him in words of favor and indulgence. She said that it was natural, after all, at his time of life, to love, and that his superior rank and station entitled him to some degree of immunity from the restrictions imposed upon ordinary men. Acte was indeed a beautiful girl, and she was not surprised, she said, that he had conceived an affection for her. The indulgence of his love was indeed attended with difficulty and danger, but, if he would submit the affair to her care and management, she could take such precautions that all would be well. She apologized for the warmth with which she had at first spoken, and attributed it to the jealous and watchful interest which a mother must always feel in all that relates to the prosperity and happiness of her son. She said, moreover, that she was now ready and willing to enter into and promote his views, and she offered him the use of certain private apartments of her own in the palace, to meet

154   NERO.   [A.D. 55

Nero rejects his mother's advances.   His treatment of her.

Acte in, saying that, by such an arrangement, and with the precautions that she could use, he could enjoy the society of his favorite whenever he pleased, without interruption and without danger.

Nero very naturally reported all this to his companions. They of course advised him not to believe any thing that his mother said, nor to trust to her in any way. "It is all," said they, "an artful device on her part to get you into her power; and no young man of pride and spirit will submit to the disgrace of being under his mother's management and control." The young profligate listened to the counsels of his associates, and rejected the overtures which his mother had made him. He continued his attachment to Acte, but kept as much as possible aloof from Agrippina.

He desired, however, if possible, to avoid an open quarrel with his mother, and so he made some effort to treat her with attention and respect, in his general bearing toward her, while he persisted in refusing to admit her to his confidence in respect to Acte. These general attentions were, however, by no means sufficient to satisfy Agrippina. The influence of Acte was what she feared, and

He makes her a present of jewelry.

she well knew that her own power was in imminent danger of being undermined and overthrown, unless she could find some means of bringing her son's connection with his favorite under her own control.   Thus the calm that seemed for a short time to reign between Nero and his mother was an armistice rather than a peace, and this armistice was brought at length to a sudden termination by an act of Nero's which he intended as an act of conciliation and kindness, but which proved to be in effect the means of awakening his mother's anger anew, and of exciting her even to a more violent exasperation than she had felt before.

It seems that among the other treasures of the imperial palace at Rome there was an extensive wardrobe of very costly female dresses and decorations, which was appropriated to the use of the wives and mothers of the emperors.   Nero conceived the idea of making a present to his mother, from this collection.   He accordingly selected a magnificent dress, and a considerable quantity of jewelry, and sent them to Agrippina.   Instead of being gratified with this gift, however, Agrippina received it as an affront,

The Jewelry.

She had been so long accustomed to consider
herself as the first personage in the imperial
household, that she regarded all such things
as rightfully her own; and she consequently
looked upon the act of Nero in formally presenting her with a small portion of these treasures, as a simple impertinence, and as intended to notify her that he considered all
that remained of the collection as his property,
and thenceforth as such subject to his exclu-

sive control.   Instead therefore of being appeased by Nero's offering she was greatly enraged by it.   The angry invectives which she uttered were duly reported to the emperor, and his indignation and resentment were aroused by them anew, and thus the breach between the mother and the son became wider than ever.

In fact Nero began to perceive very clearly that if he intended to secure for himself any thing more than the empty semblance of power, he must at once do something effectual to curb the domineering and ambitious spirit of his mother.   After revolving this subject in his mind, he finally concluded that the measure which promised to be most decisive was to dismiss a certain public officer named Pallas, who had been brought forward into public life many years before by Agrippina, and was now the chief instrument of her political power.   Pallas was the public treasurer, and he had amassed such enormous wealth by his management of the public finances, that at one time when Claudius was complaining of the impoverished condition of his exchequer, some one replied that he would soon be rich enough if he could but

induce his treasurer to receive him into part
nership.

Pallas, as has already been said, had been
originally brought forward into public life by
the influence of Agrippina, and he had always been Agrippina's chief reliance in all
her political schemes. He had aided very
effectually in promoting her marriage with
Claudius ; and had co-operated with her in
all her subsequent measures; and Nero considered him now as his mother's chief sup-
porter and ally. Nero resolved, accordingly,
to dismiss him from office; and in order to
induce him to retire peaceably, it was agreed
that no inquiry or investigation should be
made into the state of his accounts, but every
thing should be considered as balanced and
settled. Pallas acceded to this proposal.
During the whole course of his official career,
he had lived in great magnificence and splendor, and now in laying down his office, he
withdrew from the imperial palaces, at the
head of a long train of attendants, and with a
degree of pomp and parade which attracted
universal attention. The event was regarded
by the public as a declaration on the part of
Nero, that thenceforth he himself and not his

mother was to rule; and Agrippina, of course, fell at once, many degrees, from the high position which she had held in the public estimation.

She was, of course, greatly enraged, and though utterly helpless in respect to resistance, she stormed about the palace, uttering the loudest and most violent expressions of resentment and anger.

During the continuance of this paroxysm Agrippina bitterly reproached her son for what she termed his cruel ingratitude. It was altogether to her, she said, that he owed his elevation. For a long course of years she had been making ceaseless exertions, had submitted to the greatest sacrifices, and had even committed the most atrocious crimes, to raise him to the high position to which he had attained; and now, so soon as he had attained it, and had made himself sure, as he fancied, of his foothold, his first act was to turn basely and ungratefully against the hand that had raised him. But notwithstanding his fancied security, she would teach him, she said, that her power was still to be feared. Britannicus was still alive, and he was after all the rightful heir, and since her son had proved him-

self so unworthy of the efforts and sacrifices
that she had made for him, she would forthwith take measures to restore to Britannicus
what she had so unjustly taken from him.
She would immediately divulge all the dreadful secrets which were connected with Nero's
elevation. She would make known the arts
by means of which her marriage with Claudius had been effected, and the adoption of
Nero as Claudius's son and heir had been
secured. She would confess the murder of
Claudius, and the usurpation on her part of
the imperial power for Nero her son. Nero
would, in consequence, be deposed, and Britannicus would succeed him, and thus the base
ingratitude and treachery toward his mother
which Nero had displayed would be avenged.
This plan, she declared, she would immediately carry into effect. She would take Britannicus to the camp, and appeal to the army
in his name. Both Burrus and Seneca would
join her, and her undutiful and treacherous
son would be stripped forthwith of his ill-
gotten power.

These words of Agrippina were not, however, the expressions of sober purpose, really
and honestly entertained. They were the

wild and unthinking threats and denunciations which are prompted in such cases by
the frenzy of helpless and impotent rage. It
is not at all probable that she had any serious
intention of attempting such desperate measures as she threatened; for if she had really
entertained such a design, she would have
carefully kept it secret while making her arrangements for carrying it into execution.

Still these threats and denunciations, though
they were obviously prompted by a blind and
temporary rage, which it might be reasonably
supposed would soon subside, made a deep
impression upon Nero's mind. In the first
place, he was angry with his mother for daring to utter them. Then there was at least a
possibility that she might really undertake to
put them in execution, as no one could foresee what her desperate frenzy might lead
her to do. Then besides, even if Agrippina's
resentment were to subside, and she should
seem entirely to abandon all idea of ever executing her threats, Nero was extremely unwilling to remain thus in his mother's power
—exposed continually to fresh outbreaks of
her hostility, whenever her anger or her caprice might arouse her again. The threats

which his mother uttered made him, therefore, extremely restless and uneasy.

A circumstance occurred about this time
which, though very trifling in itself, had the
effect greatly to increase the jealousy and fear
in respect to Britannicus, which Nero was
inclined to feel. It seems that among the
other amusements with which the company
were accustomed to entertain themselves in
the social gatherings that took place, from
time to time, in the imperial palace, there was
a certain game which they used to play,
called, "Who shall be king?" The game
consisted of choosing one of the party by lot
to be king, and then of requiring all the others
to obey the commands, whatever they might
be, which the king so chosen might issue.
Of course, the success of the game depended
upon the art and ingenuity of the king in
prescribing such things to be done by his
various subjects, as would most entertain and
amuse the company. What the forfeit or
penalty was, that the rules of the game required, in case of disobedience, is not stated;
but every one was considered bound to obey
the commands that were laid upon him,—

provided, of course, that the thing required was within his power.

Nero himself, it appears, was accustomed to jo'n in these sports, and one evening, when a party were all playing it together in his palace, it fell to *his* lot to be king. When it came to be the turn of Britannicus to receive orders, Nero directed him to go out into the middle of the room, and sing a song to the company. This was a very severe require-ment for one so young as Britannicus, and so little accustomed to take an active part in the festivities of so gay a company ; and the mo-tive of Nero in making it, was supposed to be a feeling of ill-will, and a desire to tease his brother, by placing him in an awkward and embarrassing situation—one in which he would be compelled either to interrupt the game by refusing to obey the orders of the king, or to expose himself to ridicule by making a fruit-less attempt to sing a song.

To the surprise of all, however, Britannicus rose from his seat without any apparent hesi-tation or embarrassment, walked out upon the floor, and took his position. The attention of the whole company was fixed upon him. All sounds were hushed.

He began to sing. The song was a lament,
describing in plaintive words and in mournful
music, the situation and the sorrows of a young
prince, excluded wrongfully from the throne
of his ancestors.* The whole company listened with profound attention, charmed at first
by the artless simplicity of the music, and the
grace and beauty of the boy. As Britannicus
proceeded in his song, and the meaning of it,
in its application to his own case, began to be
perceived, a universal sympathy for him was
felt, by the whole assembly, and when he concluded and resumed his seat, the apartment

* By some it has been thought that the song which Britannicus sung on this occasion was one which he had learned
before—one perhaps which he had accidentally seen or heard,
and which had attracted his attention on account of its adapt-
edness to his own case; and there is a song of Ennius, an ancient writer, which is sometimes cited as the one he sang on
this occasion. Others say that the performance was original
and extemporaneous; that the young prince, excited by his
wrongs, and by the peculiar circumstances of the occasion,
gave utterance to his own feelings in words which suggested
themselves to him on the spot. To do this would require, of
course great intellectual readiness and ability,—but the difficulty of such a performance would be somewhat diminished
by the fact, that the ancient poetry was wholly different
from that of modern times, being marked only by a meas-
ured cadence, unconnected with rhyme

A.D. 55.]   BRITANNICUS.   165

Nero resolves to resort to poison.   Pollio and Locusta.

was filled with suppressed murmurs of applause. The effect of this scene upon the mind of Nero, was of course only to awaken feelings of vexation and anger. He looked on in moody silence, uttering mentally the fiercest threats and denunciations against the object of his jealousy, whom he was now compelled to look upon, more than ever before, as a dangerous and formidable rival. He determined, in fact, that Britannicus should die.

In considering by what means he should undertake to effect his purpose, it seemed to Nero most prudent to employ poison. There was no pretext whatever for any criminal charge against the young prince, and Nero did not dare to resort to open violence. He determined, therefore, to resort to poison, and to employ Locusta to prepare it.

Locusta, the reader will remember, was the woman whom Agrippina had employed for the murder of her husband, Claudius. She was still in custody as a convict, being under sentence of death for her crimes. She was in charge of a certain captain named Pollio, an officer of the Prætorian guard. Nero sent for Pollio, and directed him to procure from his prisoner a poisonous potion suitable for the

11

purpose intended. The potion was prepared, and soon afterward it was administered. At least it was given to certain attendants that were employed about the person of Britannicus, with orders that they should administer it. The expected effect, however, was not produced. Whether it was because the potion which Locusta had prepared was too weak, or because it was not really administered by those who received it in charge, no result followed, and Nero was greatly enraged. He sent for Pollio, and assailed him with reproaches and threats, and as for Locusta, he declared that she should be immediately put to death. They were both miserable cowards, he said, who had not the firmness to do their duty. Pollio, in reply, made the most earnest protestations of his readiness to do whatever his master should command. He assured Nero that the failure of their attempt was owing entirely to some accidental cause, and that if he would give Locusta one more opportunity to make the trial, he would guarantee that she would prepare a mixture that would kill Britannicus as quick as a dagger would do it.

Nero ordered that this should immediately

be done. Locusta was sent for, and was shut
up with Pollio in an apartment adjoining that
of the emperor, with directions to make the
mixture there, and then to administer it forthwith. Their lives were to depend upon the
result. The poison was soon prepared. There
was, however, a serious difficulty in the way
of administering it, since a potion so sudden
and violent in its character as this was intended to be, might be expected to take immediate
effect upon the taster, and so produce an alarm
which would prevent Britannicus from receiving it. To obviate this difficulty, Pollio
and Locusta cunningly contrived the following plan.

They mixed the poison when it was prepared, with cold water, and put it in the pitcher
in which cold water was customarily kept in
the apartment where Britannicus was to take
his supper. When the time arrived Nero
himself came in and took his place upon a
couch which was standing in the room, with a
view of watching the proceedings. Some
broth was brought in for the prince's supper.
The attendant whose duty it was, tasted it as
usual, and then passed it into the prince's
hand. Britannicus tasted it, and found it

too hot. It had been purposely made so.
He gave it back to the attendant to be
cooled. The attendant took it to the pitcher,
and cooled it with the poisoned water, and
then gave it back again to Britannicus without asking the taster to taste it again. Britannicus drank the broth. In a few minutes the
fatal consequences ensued. The unhappy
victim sank suddenly down in a fainting fit.
His eyes became fixed, his limbs were par-
alyzed, his breathing was short and convulsive. The attendants rushed toward him to
render him assistance, but his life was fast
ebbing away, and before they could recover
from the shock which his sudden illness occasioned them, they found that he had ceased
to breathe.

The event produced, of course, great excitement and commotion throughout the palace.
Agrippina was immediately summoned, and
as she stood over the dying child she was
overwhelmed with terror and distress. Nero,
on the other hand, appeared wholly unmoved
" It is only one of his epileptic fits," said he.
" Britannicus has been accustomed to them
from infancy He will soon recover."

As soon, however, as there was no longer

any room to question that Britannicus was dead, Nero began immediately to make preparations for the burial of the body. The remorse which, notwithstanding his depravity, he could not but feel at having perpetrated such a crime, made him impatient to remove all traces and memorials of it from his sight; and, besides, he was afraid to wait the usual period and then to make arrangements for a public funeral, lest the truth in respect to the death of Britannicus might be suspected by the Romans, and a party be formed to revenge his wrongs. Any tendency of this kind which might exist would be greatly favored, he knew, by the excitement of a public funeral. He determined, therefore, that the body should be immediately buried.

There was another reason still for this dispatch. It seems that one of the effects of the species of poison which Locusta had administered was that the body of the victim was turned black by it soon after death. This discoloration, in fact, began to appear in the face of the corpse of Britannicus before the time for the interment arrived; and Nero, in order to guard against the exposure which this phenomenon threatened, ordered the face to be painted of the natural color, by means of cosmetics, such as the ladies of the court were accustomed to use in those days. By doing this the countenance of the dead was restored to its proper color, and afterward underwent no further change. Still the emperor was naturally impatient to have the body interred.

The preparations were accordingly made that same evening, and in the middle of the night the body of Britannicus was buried in the Field of Mars, a vast parade-ground in the precincts of the city. In addition to the darkness of the night, a violent storm arose, and the rain fell in torrents while the interment proceeded. Very few, therefore, of the people of the city knew what had occurred until the following day. The violence of the storm, however, which promoted in one respect the accomplishment of Nero's designs by favoring the secrecy of the interment, in another respect operated strongly against him for the face of the corpse became so wet with the fallen rain, that the cosmetic was washed away and the blackened skin was brought to view. The attendants who had the body in charge learned thus that the boy had been poisoned.

Nero's proclamation.

On the morning after the funeral the emperor issued a proclamation announcing the death and burial of his brother, and calling upon the Roman Senate and the Roman people for their sympathy and support in the bereavement which he had sustained.

At the time of his death Britannicus was fourteen years old.

CHAPTER VIII.

THE FATE OF AGRIPPINA.

HOWEVER it may have been with others, Agrippina herself was not deceived by the false pretenses which Nero offered in explanation of his brother's death. She understood the case too well, and the event filled her mind with a tumult of conflicting emotions. Notwithstanding the terrible quarrels which had disturbed her intercourse with the emperor, he was still her son,—her first-born son,—and she loved him as such, even in the midst of the resentment and hostility which her disappointed ambition from time to time awakened in her mind. Her ambition was now more bitterly disappointed than ever. In the death of Britannicus the last link of her power over Nero seemed to be forever sundered. The hand by which he had fallen was still that of her son,—a son to whom she cóuld not but cling with maternal affection, while she felt deeply wounded at what she considered his cruel ingratitude toward her, and vexed and maddened at finding herself so hopelessly circumvented in all her schemes.

As for Nero himself, he had no longer any hope or expectation of being on good terms with his mother again. He saw clearly that her schemes and plans were wholly incompatible with his, and that in order to secure the prosperous accomplishment of his own designs he must now finish the work that he had begun, and curtail and restrict his mother's influence by every means in his power. Other persons he attempted to conciliate. He made splendid presents to the leading men of Rome, as bribes to prevent their instituting inquiries in respect to the death of Britannicus. To some he gave landed estates, to others sums of money, and others still he advanced to high offices of civil or military command. Those whom he most feared he removed from Rome, by giving them honorable and lucrative appointments in distant provinces.

In the mean time Agrippina herself was not idle. As soon as she recovered from the first shock which the death of Britannicus had occasioned her, she began to think of revenge

Within the limits and restrictions which the
suspicion and vigilance of Nero imposed upon
her, she formed a small circle of friends and
adherents, and sought out, diligently, though
secretly, all whom she supposed to be disaf-
fected to the government of Nero. She at
tached herself particularly to Octavia, who,
being the daughter of Claudius, succeeded
now, on the death of Britannicus, to whatever
hereditary rights had been vested in him.
She collected money, so far as she had power
to do so, from all the resources which remained to her, and she availed herself of every
opportunity to cultivate the acquaintance, and
court the favor, of all such officers of the army as were accessible to her influence. In a
word, she seemed to be meditating some secret scheme for retrieving her fallen fortunes,
—and Nero, who watched all her motions
with a jealous and suspicious eye, began to
be alarmed, not knowing to what desperate
extremes her resentment and ambition might
urge her.

Up to this time Agrippina had lived in the
imperial palace with Nero, forming, with her
retinue, a part of his household, and sharing
of course. in some sense, the official honors

paid to him. Nero now concluded, however, that he would remove her from this position and give her a separate establishment of her own,—making it correspond in its appointments with the secondary and subordinate station to which he intended thenceforth to confine her. He accordingly assigned to her a certain mansion in the city which had formerly been occupied by some branch of the imperial family, and removed her to it, with all her attendants. He dismissed, however, from her service, under various pretexts, such officers and adherents as he supposed were most devoted to her interests and most disposed to join with her in plots and conspiracies against him. The places of those whom he thus superseded were supplied by men on whom he could rely for subserviency to him. He diminished too the number of Agrippina's attendants and guards ; he withdrew the sentinels that had been accustomed to guard the gates of her apartments, and dismissed a certain corps of German soldiers that had hitherto served under her command, as a sort of life-guard. In a word he removed her from the scenes of imperial pomp and splendor in which she had been accustomed to move, and established her instead in the position of a private Roman lady.

The unhappy Agrippina soon found that this change in her position made a great change in respect to the degree of consideration and regard which was bestowed upon her by the public. The circle of her adherents and friends was gradually diminished. Her visitors were few. The emperor himself went sometimes to see his mother, but he came always attended with a retinue, and after a brief and formal interview, he retired as ceremoniously as he came,—thus giving to his visit the character simply of a duty of state etiquette. In a word, Agrippina found herself forsaken and friendless, and her mind gradually sank into a condition of hopeless despondency, vexation and chagrin.

Things continued in this state for some time until at length one night when Nero had been drinking and carousing at a banquet in his palace, a well-known courtier named Paris, one of the principal of Nero's companions and favorites, came into the apartment and informed the emperor with a countenance expressive of great concern, that he had tidings of the most serious moment to communicate to him. Nero withdrew from the scene of festivity to receive the communication, and was informed by Paris, that a discovery had been made of a deep-laid and dangerous plot, which Agrippina and certain accomplices of hers had formed. The object of the conspirators, as Paris alledged, was to depose Nero, and raise a certain descendant of Augustus Cæsar, named Plautus, to the supreme command, in his stead. This revolution being effected, Agrippina was to marry the new emperor, and thus be restored to her former power.

The statement which Paris made was very full in all its details. The names of the chief conspirators were given, and all the plans explained. The chief witness on whose authority the charge was made, was a celebrated woman of the court, an intimate acquaintance and visitor of Agrippina, named Silana. Silana and Agrippina had been very warm friends, but a terrible quarrel had recently broken out between them, in consequence of some interference on the part of Agrippina, to prevent a marriage, which had been partially arranged between Silana and a distinguished Roman citizen, from being carried

15—12

into effect. Silana had been exasperated by
this ill office, and the revelation which she
had made had been the result. Whether
uc: a conspiracy had really been formed,
and Silana had been induced to betray the
secret in consequence of the injury which
Agrippina had inflicted upon her in prevent-
ing her marriage, or whether she wholly invented the story under the impulse of a desperate revenge, was never fully known. The
historians of the time incline to the latter
opinion.

However this may be, Nero was greatly
alarmed at the communication which Paris
made to him. He immediately abandoned
his festivities and carousals, dismissed his
guests, and called a council of his most confidential advisers, to consider what was to be
done. He stated the case to this council, and
announced it as his determination immediately to pronounce sentence of death upon his
mother and upon Plautus, and to send officers
at once to execute the decree, as the first step
to be taken. Burrus, however, strongly dis-
suaded him from so rash a proceeding.
" These are only charges," said he, " at present. We have yet no proofs. An informer

has come to you at dead of night with this wild and improbable story, and if we take it for granted at once that it is true, and allow ourselves to act under the influence of excitement and alarm, we should afterward regret our rashness when the consequences could not be retrieved. Besides, Agrippina is your mother; and as it is the right of the humblest person in the commonwealth, when accused of crime, to be heard in answer to the accusation, it would be an atrocious crime to deprive the mother of the emperor of that privilege. Postpone, therefore, pronouncing judgment in this case until we can learn the facts more certainly. I pledge myself to execute sentence of death on Agrippina, if after a fair hearing, this charge is proved against her."

By such arguments and remonstrances as these Nero was in some degree appeased, and it was determined to postpone taking any decisive action in the emergency until the morning. As soon as it was day, Burrus and Seneca, accompanied by several attendants, who were to act as witnesses of the interview, were dispatched to the house of Agrippina to lay the charge before her and to hear what she had to say.

Agrippina was at first somewhat astonished at being summoned at so early an hour to give audience to so formidable a commission; but her proud spirit had become so fierce and desperate under the treatment which she had received from her son, that she was very slightly sensible to fear. She listened, therefore, to the heavy charge which Burrus brought against her, undismayed; and when he paused to hear her reply, instead of excusing and defending herself, and deprecating the emperor's displeasure, she commenced the most severe and angry invectives against her son, for listening for a moment to calumnies against her so wild and improbable. That Silana, who was, as she said, a dissolute and unprincipled woman, and who, consequently, could have no idea of the strength and the fidelity of maternal affection, should think it possible that a mother could form plots and conspiracies against an only son, was not strange; but that Nero himself, for whom she had made such exertions and incurred such dangers, and to whose interests she had surrendered and sacrificed every thing that could be dear to the heart of a woman—could believe such tales, and actu

ally conceive the design of murdering his
mother on the faith of them, was not to be
endured. "Does not he know well," said
she, in a voice almost inarticulate with excitement and indignation, "that, if by any
means, Britannicus, or Plautus, or any other
man were to be raised to power, my life would
be immediately forfeited in consequence of
what I have already done for him? Can he
imagine, after the deep and desperate crimes
which I have committed for his sake, in order
that I might raise him to his present power,
that I could seal my own destruction by
bringing forward any one of his rivals and
enemies to his place? Go back and tell him
this, and say, moreover, that I demand an
audience of him. I am his mother; and I
have a right to expect that he shall see me
himself, and hear what I have to say."

The commissioners whom Nero had sent
with the accusations, were somewhat astonished at receiving these angry denunciations
and invectives in reply, instead of the meek
and faltering defense which they had ex
pected. They were overawed, too, by the
lofty and passionate energy with which Agrippina had spoken. They answered her with

12

soothing and conciliatory words, and then went back to Nero, and reported the result of their interview.

Nero consented to see his mother. In his presence she assumed the same tone of proud and injured innocence, that had characterized her interview with the messengers. She scorned to enter into any vindication of herself; but *assumed* that she was innocent, and demanded that her accusers should be punished as persons guilty of the most atrocious calumny. Nero was convinced of her innocence, and yielded to her demands. Silana and two others of her accusers, were banished from Rome. Another still was punished with death.

Thus a sort of temporary and imperfect peace was once more established between Nero and his mother.

This state of things continued for about the space of three years. During this time, the public affairs of the empire, as conducted by the ministers of state and the military generals, to whom Nero intrusted them, went on with tolerable prosperity and success, while in every thing that related to personal conduct and character, the condition of the emperor

was becoming every day more and more de
plorable. He spent his days in sloth and
sensual stupor, and his nights in the wildest
riot and debauchery. He used to disguise
himself as a slave, and sally forth at mid
night with a party of his companions simi
larly attired, into the streets of the city, dis
turbing the night with riot and noise. Sometimes they would go out at an earlier hour,—
while the people were in the streets and the
shops were open,—and amuse themselves with
seizing the goods and merchandise that they
found offered for sale, and assaulting all that
came in their way. In these frolics, the emperor and his party were met sometimes by
other parties; and in the brawls which ensued
Nero was frequently handled very roughly—
his opponents not knowing who he was. At
one time he was knocked down and very seriously wounded; and in consequence of this
adventure, his face was for a long time disfigured with a scar.

Although in these orgies Nero went generally in disguise, yet as he and his companions
were accustomed afterward to boast of their
exploits, it soon became generally known to
the people of the city that their young emperor

was in the habit of mingling in these midnight brawls. Of course every wild and dissolute young man in Rome was fired with an ambition to imitate the example set him by so exalted an authority. Midnight riots became the fashion. As the parties grew larger, the brawls which occurred in the streets became more and more serious, until at last Nero was accustomed to take with him a gang of soldiers and gladiators in disguise, who were instructed to follow him within call, so as to be ready to come up instantly to his aid whenever he should require their assistance.

Year after year passed away in this manner, Nero abandoning himself all the time to the grossest sensual pleasures, and growing more and more reckless and desperate every day. His mother lived during this period in comparative seclusion. She attempted to exercise some little restraint over her son, but without success. She attached herself strongly to Octavia, the wife of Nero, and would have defended her, if she could, from the injuries and wrongs which the conduct of Nero as a husband heaped upon her.

At length the young emperor, in following his round of vicious indulgence, formed an intimacy with a certain lady of the court named Poppæa, the wife of Otho, one of Nero's companions in pleasure. Nero sent Otho away on some distant appointment, in order that he might enjoy the society of Poppæa without restraint. At length Poppæa gained so great an ascendency over the mind of the emperor as to seduce him entirely away from his duty to his wife, and she proposed that they should both be divorced and then marry one another. Nero was inclined to accede to this proposal, but Agrippina strongly opposed it. For a time Nero hesitated between the influence of Agrippina and the sentiment of duty, on the one hand, and the enticements of Poppæa on the other. In addition to the influence of her blandishments and smiles, she attempted to act upon Nero's boyish pride by taunting him with what she called his degrading and unmanly subjection to his mother. How long, she asked, was he to remain like a child under maternal tutelage? She wondered how ne could endure so ignoble a bondage. He was in name and position, she said, a mighty monarch, reigning absolutely over half the world,—but in actual fact he was a mere nursery boy, who

could do nothing without his mother's leave.
She was ashamed, she said, to see him in
so humiliating a condition; and unless he
would take some vigorous measures to free
himself from his chains, she declared that she
would leave him forever, and go with her
husband to some distant quarter of the world
where she could no longer be a witness of his
disgrace.

The effect of these taunts upon the mind of
Nero was very much heightened by the proud
and imperious spirit which his mother manifested toward him, and which seemed to become more and more stern and severe, through
the growing desperation which the conduct
of her son and her own hopeless condition
seemed to awaken in her mind. The quarrel,
in a word, between the emperor and his
mother grew more and more inveterate and
hopeless every day. At length he shunned
her entirely, and finally, every remaining
spark of filial duty having become extin-
guished, he began to meditate some secret
plan of removing her out of his way.

He revolved various projects for accomplishing this purpose, in his mind. He did
not dare to employ open violence, as he had

no charge against his mother to justify a criminal sentence against her; and he dreaded the effect upon the public mind which would be produced by the spectacle of so unnatural a deed as the execution of a mother by command of her son. He could not trust to poison. Agrippina was perfectly familiar with every thing relating to the poisoning art, and would doubtless be fully on her guard against any attempt of that kind that he might make. Besides, he supposed, that by means of certain antidotes which she was accustomed to use, her system was permanently fortified against the action of every species of poison.

While Nero was revolving these things in his mind, the occasion occurred for a great naval celebration at Baiæ, a beautiful bay south of Rome, near what is now the bay of Naples. Baiæ was celebrated in ancient times, as it is in fact now, for the beauty of its situation, and it was a place of great resort for the Roman nobility. There was a small, but well-built town at the head of the bay, and the hills and valleys in the vicinity, as well as every headland and promontory along the shore, were ornamented with villas and country-seats, which were occupied as summer residences by the wealthy people of the city. Baiæ was also a great naval station, and there was at this time a fleet stationed there,—or rather at the promontory of Misenum, a few miles beyond,—under the command of one of Nero's confidential servants, named Anicetus. The naval celebration was to take place in connection with this fleet. It was an annual festival, and was to continue five days.

Anicetus had been a personal attendant upon Nero in his infancy, and had lived always in habits of great intimacy with him. For some reason or other, too, he was a great enemy to Agrippina, having been always accustomed, when Nero was a child, to take his part in the little contests which had arisen, from time to time, between him and his mother. Anicetus was of course prepared to sympathize very readily with Nero in the hatred which he now cherished toward Agrippina, and when he learned that Nero was desirous of devising some means of accomplishing her death, he formed a plan which he said would effect the purpose very safely. He proposed to invite Agrippina to Baiæ, and then, in the course of the ceremonies and manœuvers connected with the naval spectacle, to take her out upon the bay in a barge or galley. He would have the barge so constructed, he said, that it should go to pieces at sea, making arrangements beforehand for saving the lives of the others, but leaving Agrippina to be drowned.

Nero was greatly pleased with this device, and determined at once to adopt the plan. In order to open the way for carrying it into effect, he pretended, when the time for the festival drew nigh, that he desired to be reconciled to his mother, and that he was ready now to fall in with her wishes and plans. He begged her to forget all his past unkindness to her, and assuring her that his feelings toward her were now wholly changed, he lavished upon her expressions of the tenderest regard. A mother is always very easily deceived by such protestations on the part of a wayward son, and Agrippina believed all that Nero said to her. In a word, the reconciliation seemed to be complete.

At length, when the time for the naval festival drew nigh, Nero, who was then at Baiæ, sent an invitation to his mother to come and join him in witnessing the spectacle. Agrippina readily consented to accept the invita

tion. She was at this time at Antium, the
place, it will be recollected, where Nero was
born. She accordingly set sail from this place
in her own galley, and proceeded to the
southward. She landed at one of the villas
in the neighborhood of Baiæ. Nero was ready
upon the shore to meet her. He received her
with every demonstration of respect and affection. He had provided quarters for her at
Baiæ, and there was a splendid barge ready
to convey her thither; the plan being that
she should embark on board this barge, and
leave her own galley,—that is the one by
which she had come in from sea,—at anchor
at the villa where she landed. The barge in
which Agrippina was thus invited to embark,
was the treacherous trap that Anicetus had
contrived for her destruction. It was, however, to all appearance, a very splendid vessel, being very richly and beautifully deco-
rated, as if expressly intended to do honor to
the distinguished passenger whom it was designed to convey.

Agrippina, however, did not seem inclined
to go in the barge. She preferred proceeding
to Baiæ by land. Perhaps, notwithstanding
Nero's apparent friendliness she felt still

some misgivings, and was afraid to trust herself entirely to his power,—or perhaps she
preferred to finish her journey by land only
because, in making the passage from Antium,
she had become tired of the sea. However
this may have been, Nero acquiesced at once
in her decision, and provided a sort of sedan
for conveying her to Baiæ by land. In this
sedan she was carried accordingly, by bearers
to Baiæ, and there lodged in the apartments
provided for her.

No favorable opportunity occurred for
taking Agrippina out upon the water until
the time arrived for her return to Antium.
During the time of her stay at Baiæ, Nero
devoted himself to her with the most assiduous attention. He prepared magnificent
banquets for her, and entertained her with a
great variety of amusements and diversions.
In his conversation he sometimes addressed
her with a familiar playfulness and gayety,
and at other times he sought occasions to dis-
course with her seriously on public affairs, in
a private and confidential manner. Agrippina was completely deceived by these indications, and her heart was filled with pride

and joy at the thought that she had regained the affection and confidence of her son.

Nero and Anicetus determined finally to put their plan into execution by inducing Agrippina to embark on board their barge in returning to Antium, when the time should arrive, instead of going back in her own vessel. Their other attempts to induce her to go out upon the water had failed, and this was the only opportunity that now remained. It was desirable that this embarkation should take place in the night, as the deed which they were contemplating could be more effectually accomplished under the cover of the darkness. Accordingly, on the afternoon of the day on which Agrippina was to return, Nero prepared a banquet for her, and he protracted the festivities and entertainments which attended it until late in the evening, so that it was wholly dark before his mother could take her leave. Anicetus then contrived to have one of the vessels of his fleet run against the galley in which Agrippina had come from Antium, as it lay at anchor near the shore at the place where she had landed. The galley was broken down and disabled by the collision. Anicetus came to

Nero bids his mother an affectionate farewell.

Agrippina to report the accident, with a countenance expressive of much concern; but added that the barge which the emperor had prepared for her was at her service, and proposed to substitute that in the place of the one which had been injured. There seemed to be no other alternative, and Agrippina, after taking a very affectionate leave of her son, went gayly, and wholly unconscious of danger, on board the beautiful but treacherous vessel.

It was observed that Nero exhibited an extreme degree of tender regard for his mother in bidding her farewell on this occasion. He hung upon her neck a long time, and kissed her again and again, detaining her by these endearments on the shore, as if reluctant to let her go. After Agrippina's death this scene was remembered by those who witnessed it, but in reflecting upon it they could not decide whether these tokens of affection were all assumed, as belonging to the part which he was so hypocritically acting, or whether he really felt at the last moment some filial relentings, which led him to detain his mother for a time on the brink of the pit which he had been preparing for her destruction. From

15—13

all, however, that we now know in respect to
the personal character which Nero had formed
at this period, it is probable that the former
is the correct supposition.

The plot, dextrous as the contrivance of it
had been, was not destined to succeed. The
vessel moved gently from the shore, rowed by
the mariners. It was a clear starlight night.
The sea was smooth, and the air was calm
Agrippina took her place upon a couch which
had been arranged for her, under a sort of
canopy or awning, the frame-work of which,
above, had been secretly loaded with lead.
She was attended here by one of her ladies
named Aceronia Polla, who lay at her mistress's feet, and entertained her with conversation as the boat glided along on its way.
They talked of Nero—of the kind attentions
which he had been paying to Agrippina, and
of the various advantages which were to follow from the reconciliation which had been
so happily effected. In this manner the hours
passed away, and the barge went on until it
reached the place which had been determined
upon for breaking it down and casting Agrip
pina into the sea. The spot which had been
chosen was so near the land as to allow of the

escape of the mariners by swimming, but yet remote enough, as was supposed, to make Agrippina's destruction sure. A few of the mariners were in the secret, and were in some degree prepared for what was to come. Others knew nothing, and were expected to save themselves as they best could, when they should find themselves cast into the sea.

At a given signal the fastenings of the canopy were loosened, and the loaded structure came down suddenly with a heavy crash, carrying away with it other parts of the vessel. One man was crushed under the weight of the falling ruins, and instantly killed. Agrippina and the lady in waiting upon her were saved by the posts of the bed or couch on which Agrippina was reclining, which happened to be in such a position that they held up the impending mass sufficiently to allow the ladies to creep out from beneath it. The breaking down, too, of the deck and bulwarks of the barge was less extensive than had been intended, so that Agrippina not only escaped being crushed by the ruins but she also saved herself at first from being thrown into the sea. The men then who were in the secret of the plot immediately raised a great cry and con-

fusion, and attempted to upset the barge by
climbing up upon one side of it—while the
others, who did not understand the case, did
all they could to save it. In the mean time
the noise of the outcries reached the shore,
and fishermen's boats began to put off with a
view of coming to the rescue of the distressed
vessel. Before they arrived, however, the
boat had been overturned, Agrippina and
Aceronia had been thrown into the sea, and
the men who were in the secret of the plot,
taking advantage of the darkness and confusion, were endeavoring to seal the fate of
their victims, by beating them down with
poles and oars as they struggled in the water.

These efforts succeeded in the case of Aceronia, for she uttered loud and continual outcries in her terror, and thus drew upon herself the blows of the assassins. Agrippina,
on the other hand, had the presence of mind
to keep silence. She received one heavy blow
upon the shoulder, which inflicted a serious
wound. In other respects she escaped unin-
jured, and succeeded, partly through the
buoyancy of her dress, and partly by the ef
forts that she made to swim, in keeping her
self afloat until she was taken up by the fish

LOSSING—BARRITT

THE ATTEMPT OF ANICETUS.

ermen and conveyed to the shore. She was
taken to a villa belonging to her, which was
situated not far from the place where the dis-
aster had occurred.

As soon as Agrippina had recovered a little
from the terror and excitement of this scene,
and had time to reflect upon the circumstances of it, she was convinced that what had
occurred was no accident, but the result of a
deep-laid design to destroy her life. She,
however, thought it most prudent to dissem-
ble her opinion for a time. As soon therefore
as she had safely reached her villa, and her
wound had been dressed, she dispatched a
messenger to Baiæ to inform Nero of what
had occurred. The vessel in which she had
embarked had been wrecked at sea, she said,
and she had narrowly escaped destruction.
She had received a severe hurt, by some falling spar, but had at length safely reached her
home at Antium. She begged, however, that
her son would not come to see her, as what
she needed most was repose. She had sent
the messenger, she said, to inform him of
what had occurred only that he might rejoice
with her in the signal interposition of divine

providence by which she had been rescued from so imminent a danger.

In the mean time Nero was waiting impatiently and anxiously in his palace at Baiæ, for the arrival of a messenger from Anicetus to inform him that his plot had been successful, and that his mother was drowned. Instead of this a rumor of her escape reached him some time before Agrippina's messenger arrived, and threw him into consternation. People came from the coast and informed him that the barge in which his mother had sailed had been wrecked, and that Agrippina had narrowly escaped with her life. . The particulars were not fully given to him, but he presumed that Agrippina must have learned that the occurrence was the result of a deliberate attempt to destroy her, and he was consequently very much alarmed. He dreaded the desperate spirit of resentment and revenge which he presumed had been aroused in his mother's mind.

He forthwith sent for Burrus and Seneca, and revealed to them all the circumstances of the case. He made the most bitter accusations against his mother, in justification of his attempt to destroy her. He had long been

convinced, he said, that there could be no
peace or safety for him as long as she lived,
and now, at all events, since he had undertaken the work of destroying her and made
the attempt, no alternative was left to him but
to go on and finish what he had begun. "She
must die now," said he, "or she will most as-
suredly contrive some means to destroy me."

Seneca and Burrus were silent. They
knew not what to say. They saw very clearly
that a crisis had arrived, the end of which
would be, that one or the other must perish,
and consequently the only question for them
to decide was, whether the victim should be
the mother or the son. At length, after a
long and solemn pause, Seneca looked to
Burrus, and inquired whether the soldiers
under his command could be relied upon
to execute death upon Agrippina. Burrus
shook his head. The soldiers, he said, felt
such a veneration for the family of Germanicus, which was the family from which Agrippina had sprung, that they would perform no
such bloody work upon any representative of
it. "Besides," said he, "Anicetus has undertaken this duty. It devolves on him to
finish what he has begun."

Anicetus readily undertook the task. He
had, in fact, a personal interest in it; for,
after what had passed, he knew well that
there could be no safety for him while Agrip
pina lived. Nero seemed overjoyed at finding Anicetus so ready to meet his wishes.
" Be prompt," said he, " in doing what you
have to do. Take with you whom you please
to assist you. If you accomplish the work, I
shall consider that I owe my empire to your
fidelity."

Anicetus, having thus received his commission, ordered a small detachment from the
fleet to accompany him, and proceeded to the
villa where Agrippina had taken refuge. He
found a crowd of country people assembled
around the gates of the villa. They had
been drawn thither by the tidings of the dis-
aster which had happened to Agrippina, curious to learn all the particulars of the occurrence, or desirous, perhaps, to congratulate
Agrippina on her escape. When these peas-
antry saw the armed band of Anicetus ap
proaching, they know not what it meant,
but were greatly alarmed, and fled in all
directions.

The guards at the gates of Agrippina's

villa made some resistance to the entrance of
the soldiers, but they were soon knocked
down and overpowered; the gates were burst
open, and Anicetus entered at the head of
his party of marines. Agrippina, who was
upon her bed in an inner chamber at the time,
heard the noise and tumult, and was greatly
alarmed. A number of friends who were
with her, hearing the footsteps of the armed
men on the stairs, fled from the chamber in
dismay, by a private door, leaving Agrippina
alone with her maid. The maid, after a moment's pause, fled too, Agrippina saying to
her as she disappeared, " Are you, too, going
to forsake me?" At the same moment, Anicetus forced open the door of entrance, and
came in accompanied by two of his officers.
The three armed men, with an expression of
fierce and relentless determination upon their
countenances, advanced to Agrippina's bed
side.

Agrippina was greatly terrified, but she
preserved some degree of outward composure,
and raising herself in her bed, she looked
steadily upon her assassins.

" Do you come from my son?" said she.

They did not answer.

"If you came to inquire how I am," said
she, "tell him that I am better, and shall
oon be entirely well. I can not believe that
e can possibly have sent you to do me any
violence or harm."

At this instant one of the assassins struck
at the wretched mother with his club. The
arm, however, of the most hardened and un-
relenting monster, usually falters somewhat
at the beginning, in doing such work as this,
and the blow gave Agrippina only an incon-
siderable wound. She saw at once, however,
that all was lost—that the bitter moment of
death had come,—but instead of yielding to
the emotions of terror and despair which
might have been expected to overwhelm the
heart of a woman in such a scene, her fierce
and indomitable spirit aroused itself to new
life and vigor in the terrible emergency.
As the assassins approached her with their
swords brandished in the air, preparing to
strike her, she threw the bed-clothes off, so
as to uncover her person, and called upon her
murderers to strike her in the womb. "It is
there," said she, "that the stab should be
given when a mother is to be murdered by
her son." She was instantly thrust through

with a multitude of wounds in every part of her body, and died weltering in the blood that flowed out upon the couch on which she lay.

Anicetus and his comrades, when the deed was done, gazed for a moment on the lifeless body, and then gathering together again the soldiers that they had left at the gates, they went back to Baiæ with the tidings. The first emotion which Nero experienced, on hearing that all was over, was that of relief. He soon found, however, that monster as he was, his conscience was not yet so stupefied, that he could perpetrate such a deed as this without bringing out her scourge. As soon as he began to reflect upon what he had done, his soul was overwhelmed with remorse and horror. He passed the remainder of the night in dreadful agony, sometimes sitting silent and motionless—gazing into vacancy, as if his faculties were bewildered and lost, and then suddenly starting up, amazed and trembling, and staring wildly about, as if seized with a sudden frenzy. His wild and ghastly looks, his convulsive gesticulations, and his incoherent ravings and groans, indicated the horror that he endured, and were so frightful that his officers and attendants shrunk away from his presence, and knew not what to do.

At length they sent in one after another to attempt to calm and console him. Their efforts, however, were attended with little success. When the morning came, it brought with it some degree of composure; but the dreadful burden of guilt which pressed upon Nero's mind made him still unutterably wretched. He said that he could not endure any longer to remain on the spot, as every thing that he saw, the villas, the ships, the sea, the shore, and all the other objects around him, were so associated in his mind with the thought of his mother, and with the remembrance of his dreadful crime, that he could not endure them.

In the mean time, as soon as the servants and attendants at Agrippina's villa found that Anicetus and his troop had gone, they returned to the chamber of their mistress and gazed upon the spectacle which awaited them there, with inexpressible horror. Anicetus had left some of his men behind to attend to the disposal of the body, as it was important that it should be removed from sight without delay, since it might be expected that all

Burning of the body of Agrippina.

who should look upon it would be excited to a high pitch of indignation against the perpetrators of such a crime. The countenance, in the condition of repose which it assumed after death, appeared extremely beautiful, and seemed to address a mute but touching appeal to the commiseration of every beholder. It was necessary, therefore, to hurry it away. Besides, the soldiers themselves were impatient. They wished to get through with their horrid work and be gone.

They accordingly built a funeral pile in the garden of the villa,—using such materials for the purpose as came most readily to hand—and then took up the body of Agrippina on the bed upon which it lay, and placed all together upon the pile. The fires were lighted. The soldiers watched by the side of it until the pile was nearly consumed, and then went away, leaving the heart-broken domestics of Agrippina around the smoldering embers.

CHAPTER IX.

EXTREME DEPRAVITY.

THERE was nothing in the attendant circumstances that were connected with the act of Nero in murdering his mother, which could palliate or extenuate the deed in the slightest degree. It was not an act of self-defense. Agrippina was not doing him, or intending to do him any injury. It was not an act of hasty violence, prompted by sudden passion. It was not required by any political necessity as a means for accomplishing some great and desirable public end. It was a cool, deliberate, and well-considered crime, performed solely for the purpose of removing from the path of the perpetrator of it an obstacle to the commission of another crime. Nero murdered his mother in cool blood, simply because she was in the way of his plans for divorcing his innocent wife, and marrying adulterously another woman.

For some time after the commission of this

great crime, the mind of Nero was haunted
by dreadful fears, and he suffered continually,
by day and by night, all the pangs of remorse
and horror. He did not dare to return to
Rome, not knowing to what height the popular indignation, that would be naturally ex
cited by so atrocious a deed, might rise ; or
what might be the consequences to him if he
were to appear in the city. He accordingly
remained for a time on the coast at Neapolis.
the town to which he had retired from Baiæ.
From this place he sent various communications to the Roman Senate, explaining and
justifying what he called the execution of his
mother. He pretended that he had found her
guilty of treasonable conspiracies against him
and against the state, and that her death had
been imperiously demanded, as the only
means of securing the public safety. The
senators hated Nero and abhorred his crimes ;
but they were overawed by the terrible power
which he exercised over them through the
army, which they knew was entirely subservient to his will, and by their dread of his
ruthless and desperate character. They passed resolves approving of what he had done.
His officers and favorites at Rome sent him

word that the memory of Agrippina was abhorred at the capital, and that in destroying ner, he was considered as having rendered a great service to the state. These representations in some measure reassured his mind, and at length he returned to the city.

In due time he divorced Octavia, and married Poppæa. Octavia, however, still remained at Rome, residing in apartments assigned her in one of the imperial palaces. Her high birth and distinguished position, and, more than all, the sympathy that was felt for her in her misfortunes, made her an object of great attention. The people put garlands upon her statues in the public places in the city, and pulled down those which were placed at Nero's command upon those of Poppæa. These and other indications of the popular feeling, inflamed Poppæa's hatred and jealousy to such a degree, that she suborned one of Octavia's domestics to accuse her mistress of an ignominious crime. When thus accused, other women in Octavia's service were put to the rack to compel them to testify against her They, however, persevered, in the midst of their tortures, in asserting her innocence. Poppæa, nevertheless, insisted that she should be condemned, and at last, by way of compromising the case, Nero consented to banish her from the city.

She was sent to a villa on the sea-coast, in the neighborhood of the place where Anicetus was stationed with his fleet. But Poppæa would not allow her to live in peace even as an exile. She soon brought a charge against her of having formed a conspiracy against the government of Nero, and of having corrupted Anicetus, with a view of obtaining the co-operation of the fleet in the execution of trea sonable designs. Anicetus himself testified to the truth of this charge. He said that Oc tavia had formed such a plan, and that she had given herself up, in person, wholly to him, in order to induce him to join in it. Oc tavia was accordingly condemned to die.

Notwithstanding the testimony of Anicetus, Octavia was not at the time generally believed to be guilty of the charge on which she was condemned. It was supposed that Anicetus was induced, by promises and bribes from Nero and Poppæa, to fabricate the story, in order that they might have a pretext for put ting Octavia to death. However this may be, the unhappy princess was condemned, and the sentence pronounced upon her was, that she must die.

The life of Octavia, lofty as her position was in respect to earthly grandeur, had been one of uninterrupted suffering and sorrow. She had been married to Nero when a mere child, and during the whole period of her connection with her husband he had treated her with continual unkindness. and neglect. She had at length been cruelly divorced from him, and banished from her native city on charges of the most ignominious nature, though wholly false—and before this last accusation was made against her there seemed to be nothing before her but the prospect of spending the remainder of her days in a miserable and hopeless exile. Still she clung to life, and when the messengers of Nero came to tell her that she must die, she was overwhelmed with agitation and terror.

She begged and implored them with tears and agony, to spare her life. She would never, she said, give the emperor any trouble, or interfere in any way with any of his plans. She gave up willingly all claims to being his wife and would always consider herself as only his sister. She would live in retirement

and seclusion in any place where Nero might
appoint her abode, and would never occasion
him the slightest uneasiness whatever. The
executioners cut short these entreaties by
seizing the unhappy princess in the midst of
them, binding her limbs with thongs, and
opening her veins. She fainted, however,
under this treatment, and when the veins were
opened the wretched victim lay passive and
insensible in the hands of her executioners,
and the blood would not flow. So they carried her to a steam-bath which happened to
be in readiness near at hand, and shutting
her up in it, left her to be suffocated by the
vapor.

Thus the great crowning crime of Nero's
life,—for the murder of Agrippina, the adulterous marriage with Poppæa, and the subsequent murder of Octavia, are to be regarded
as constituting one single though complicated
crime,—was consummate and complete. It
was a crime of the highest possible atrocity.
To open the way to an adulterous marriage
by the deliberate and cruel murder of a mother, and then to seal and secure it by murdering an innocent wife,—blackening her
memory at the same time with an ignominy

14

wholly undeserved, constitute a crime which
for unnatural and monstrous enormity must
be considered as standing at the head of all
that human depravity has ever achieved.

Nero gradually recovered from the remorse
and horror with which the commission of
these atrocities at first overwhelmed him;
and in order to hasten his relief he plunged
recklessly into every species of riot and excess, and in the end hardened himself so
completely in crime, that during the remainder of his life he perpetrated the most abomi-
nable deeds without any apparent compunc-
tion whatever.   He killed Poppæa herself at
last with a kick, which he gave her in a fit of
passion at a time when circumstances were
such with her that the violence brought on a
premature and unnatural sickness.   He afterward ordered her son to be drowned in the
sea, by his slaves, when he was a fishing, because he understood that the boy, in playing
with the other children, often acted the part
of an emperor.   His general Burrus he poisoned.   He sent him the poison under pretense that it was a medical remedy for a
swelling of the throat under which Burrus
was suffering.   Burrus drank the draught

under that impression and died. He destroyed by similar means in the course of his life great numbers of his relatives and officers of state, so that there was scarcely a person who was brought into any degree of intimate connection with him that did not sooner or later come to a violent end.

During his whole reign Nero neglected the public affairs of the empire almost altogether, ––apparently regarding the vast power, and the immense resources that were at his command, as only means for the more complete gratification of his own personal propensities and passions. The only ambition which ever appeared to animate him was a desire for fame as a singer and actor on the stage.

At the time when he commenced his career it was considered wholly beneath the dignity of any Roman of rank to appear in any public performance of that nature; but Nero, having conceived in his youth a high idea of his merit as a singer, devoted himself with great assiduity to the cultivation of his voice, and, as he was encouraged in what he did by the flatterers that of course were always around him, his interest in the musical art became at length an extravagant passion. He

submitted with the greatest patience to the
rigorous training customary in those times
for the development and improvement of the
voice; such as lying for long periods upon
his back, with a weight of lead upon his
breast, in order to force the muscles of the
chest to extraordinary exertion, for the purpose of strengthening them—and taking medicines of various kinds to clear the voice and
reduce the system. He was so much pleased
with the success of these efforts, that he began to feel a great desire to perform in public
upon the stage. He accordingly began to
make arrangements for doing this. He first
appeared in private exhibitions, in the imperial palaces and gardens, where only the
nobility of Rome and invited guests were
present. He, however, gradually extended
his audiences, and at length came out upon
the public stage,—first, however, in order to
prepare the public mind for what they would
have otherwise considered a great degradation,
inducing the sons of some of the principal
nobility to come forward in similar entertainments. He was so pleased with the success
which he imagined that he met with in this
career that he devoted a large part of his

time during his whole life to such performances. Of course, his love of applause in his
theatrical career, increased much too fast to
be satisfied with the natural and ordinary
means of gratifying it, and he accordingly
made arrangements, most absurdly, to create
for his performances a fictitious and counter-
feit celebrity. At one time he had a corps
of five thousand men under pay to applaud
him, in the immense circuses and amphitheaters where he performed. These men were
regularly trained to the work of applauding,
as if it were an art to be acquired by study
and instruction. It *was* an art, in fact, as
they practiced it,—different modes of ap
plause being designated for different species
of merit, and the utmost precision being required on the part of the performers, in the
concert of their action, and in their obedience
to the signals. He used also to require on
the days when he was to perform, that the
doors of the theater should be closed when
the audience had assembled, and no egress
allowed on any pretext whatever. Such regulations of course excited great complaint,
and much ridicule; especially as the sessions
at these spectacles were sometimes protracted

and tiresome to the last degree. Even sudden sickness was not a sufficient reason for allowing a spectator to depart, and so it was said that the people used sometimes to feign death, in order to be carried out to their burial. In some cases, it was said, births took place in the theaters, the mothers having come incautiously with the crowd to witness the spectacles, without properly considering what might be the effect of the excitement, and then afterward not being permitted to retire.

Besides singing and acting on the stage, Nero took part in every other species of public amusement. He entered as a competitor for the prize in races and games of every kind. Of course he always came off victor. This end was accomplished sometimes by the secret connivance of the other competitors, and sometimes by open bribery of the judges. Nero's ridiculous vanity and self-conceit seemed to be fully gratified by receiving the prize, without any regard whatever to the question of deserving it. He used to come back sometimes from journeys to foreign cities, where he had been performing on the stage at great public festivals, and enter Rome in triumph, with the garlands, and crowns, and other decorations which he had won, paraded before him in the procession, in the manner in which distinguished commanders had been accustomed to display the trophies of their military victories, when returning from foreign campaigns.

In fact it was only in the perpetration of such miserable follies as these that Nero appeared before the public at all, and in his private conduct and character he sank very rapidly, after he came into power, to the very lowest degree of profligacy and vice. After having spent the evening in drinking and debauchery, he would sally forth into the streets at midnight, as has already been stated, to mingle there with the vilest men and women of the town in brawls and riots. On these excursions he would attack such peaceable parties as he chanced to meet in the streets, and if they made resistance, he and his companions would beat them down and throw them into canals or open sewers. Sometimes in these combats he was beaten himself, and on one occasion he came very near losing his life, having been almost killed by the blows dealt upon him by a certain Roman senator

whose wife he insulted as she was walking
with her husband in the street. The senator,
of course, did not know him. He used to go
to the theater in disguise, in company with a
gang of companions of similar character to
himself, and watch for opportunities to excite
or encourage riots or tumults there. Whenever he could succeed in urging these tumults
on to actual violence he would mingle in the
fray, and throw stones and fragments of
broken benches and furniture among the
people.

After a while, when he had grown more
bold and desperate in his wickedness, he began to lay aside all disguise, and at last he
actually seemed to take a pride and pleasure
in exhibiting the scenes of riot and excess in
which he engaged, in the most impudent
manner before the public gaze. He used to
celebrate great feasts in the public amphitheaters, and on the arena of the circus, and ca-
rouse there in company with the most disso
lute men and women of the city—a spectacle
to the whole population. There was a large
artificial lake or reservoir in one part of the
city, built for the purpose of exhibiting
mimic representations of the manœuvers of

fleets, and naval battles, for the amusement
of the people at great public celebrations.
There were, of course, numerous ranges of
seats around the margin of this lake for the
accommodation of the spectators. Nero took
possession of this structure for some of his
carousals, in order to obtain greater scope for
ostentation and display. The water was
drawn off on such occasions and the gates
shut, and then the bottom of the reservoir
was floored over to make space for the tables.

The sums of money which Nero spent in
the pursuit of sensual pleasures were incalcu-
lable. In fact there were no bounds to his
extravagance and profusion. He had command, of course, of all the treasure of the empire, and he procured immense sums besides,
by fines, confiscations, and despotic exactions
of various kinds ; and as he undertook no
public enterprises—being seldom engaged in
foreign wars, and seldom attempting any useful constructions in the city—the vast resources at his command were wholly devoted
to the purposes of ostentatious personal display, and sensual gratifications. The pomp
and splendor of his feasts, his processions, his
journeys of pleasure, and the sums that he is

said to have lavished sometimes in money and jewels, and sometimes in villas, gardens, and equipages, upon his favorites, both male and female, are almost incredible. On some of the pleasure excursions which he took to the mouth of the Tiber, he would have the banks of the river lined with booths and costly tents all the way from the river to the sea. These tents were provided with sumptuous entertainments, and with beds and couches for repose ; and they were all attended by beautiful girls who stood at the doors of them inviting Nero and his party to land, as they passed along the river in their barges. He used to fish with a golden net, which was drawn by silken cords of a rich scarlet color. Occasionally he made grand excursions of pleasure through Italy or into Greece, in the style of royal progresses. In these expeditions he sometimes had no less than a thousand carts to convey his baggage—the mules that drew them being all shod with silver, and their drivers dressed in scarlet clothes of the most costly character. He was attended, also, on these excursions, by a numerous train of footmen, and of African servants, who wore rich bracelets upon their arms, and were mounted on horses splendidly caparisoned.

One of the most remarkable of the events which occurred during Nero's reign was what was called the burning of Rome,—a great conflagration, by which a large part of the city was destroyed. It was very generally believed at the time that this destruction was the work of Nero himself,—the fruit of his reckless and willful depravity. There is, it is true, no very positive proof that the fire was set by Nero's orders, though one of the historians of the time states that confidential servants belonging to Nero's household were seen, when the fire commenced, going from house to house with combustibles and torches, spreading the flames. He was himself at Antium at the time, and did not come to Rome until the fire had been raging for many days. If it is true that the fire was Nero's work, it is not supposed that he designed to cause so extensive a conflagration. He intended, perhaps, only to destroy a few buildings that covered ground which he wished to occupy for the enlargement of his palaces; though it was said by some writers that he really designed to destroy a great part of the city, with a view to immortalize his name by rebuilding it in a new and more splendid form. With these motives, if these indeed were his motives, there was doubtless mingled a feeling of malicious gratification at any thing that would terrify and torment the miserable subjects of his power. When he came to Rome from Antium at the time that the conflagration was at its height, he found the whole city a scene of indescribable terror and distress. Thousands of the people had been burned to death or crushed beneath the ruins of the fallen houses. The streets were filled with piles of goods and furniture burnt and broken. Multitudes of men, though nearly exhausted with fatigue, were desperately toiling on, in hopeless endeavors to extinguish the flames, or to save some small remnant of their property,—and distracted mothers, wild and haggard from terror and despair, were roaming to and fro, seeking their children,— some moaning in anguish, and some piercing the air with loud and frantic outcries. Nero was entertained by the scene as if it had been a great dramatic spectacle. He went to one of the theaters, and taking his place upon the stage he amused himself there with singing

BURNING OF ROME.

and playing a celebrated composition on the subject of the burning of Troy. At least it was said and generally believed in the city hat he did so, and the minds of the people were excited against the inhuman monster to the highest pitch of indignation. In fact, Nero seems to have thought at last that he had gone too far, and he began to make efforts in earnest to relieve the people from some portion of their distress. He caused great numbers of tents to be erected in the parade-ground for temporary shelter, and brought fresh supplies of corn into the city to save the people from famine. These measures of mercy, however, came too late to retrieve his character. The people attributed the miseries of this dreadful calamity to his desperate maliciousness, and he became the object of universal execration.

CHAPTER X.

PISO'S CONSPIRACY.

ALTHOUGH the people of Rome were generally so overawed by the terror of Nero's power, that for a long period no one dared to make any open resistance to his will, still his excesses and cruelties excited in the minds of men a great many secret feelings of resentment and detestation. At one period in the course of his reign a very desperate conspiracy was formed by some of the leading men of the state, to dethrone and destroy the tyrant. This plot was a very extensive and a very formidable one. It was, however, accidentally discovered before it was fully mature, and thus was unsuccessful. It is known in history as Piso's Conspiracy—deriving its name from that of the principal leader of it, Caius Calpurnius Piso.

It is not supposed, however, that Piso was absolutely the originator of the conspiracy, nor is it known, in fact, who the originator of it was. A great number of prominent men

were involved in the plot—men who, possess-
ing very different characters, and occupying
very different stations in life, were probably
induced by various motives to take part in the
conspiracy. A conspiracy, however, of this
kind, against so merciless a tyrant as Nero, is
an enterprise of such frightful danger, and is
attended, if unsuccessful, with such awful
consequences to all concerned in it, that men
will seldom engage in such a scheme until
goaded to desperation, and almost maddened,
by the wrongs which they have endured.

And yet the exasperation which these conspirators felt against Nero, seems to have been
produced, in some instances at least, by what
we should now consider rather inadequate
causes. For example, one of the men most
active in this secret league, was the celebrated
Latin poet Lucan. In the early part of his
life, Lucan had been one of Nero's principal
flatterers, having written hymns and sonnets
in his praise. At length, as it was said, some
public occasion occurred in which verses were
to be recited in public, for a prize. Nero,
who imagined himself to excel in every human art or attainment, offered some of his own
verses in the competition. The prize, how-

15

ever, was adjudged to Lucan. Nero's mind was accordingly filled with envy and hate toward his rival, and he soon found some pretext for forbidding Lucan ever to recite any verses in public again. This of course exasperated Lucan in his turn, and was the cause of his joining in the conspiracy.

Another of the conspirators was a certain Roman nobleman, whose family name has since become very widely known in all parts of the civilized world, through an estate in the city with which it was associated,—which estate, and certain buildings erected upon it, became subsequently greatly celebrated in the ecclesiastical history of Rome. The name of this nobleman was Plautius Lateranus. When Lateranus was put to death at the detection of the conspiracy, in the manner to be presently described, his estate was confiscated. The palace and grounds thus became the property of the Roman emperors. In process of time, the emperor Constantine gave the place to the pope, and from that period it continued to be the residence of the successive pontiffs for a thousand years. A church was built upon the ground, called the Basilica of St. John of Lateran, where many ancient councils were

The church of St. John Lateran.

held, known in ecclesiastical history as the councils of the Lateran. This church is still used for some of the ceremonies connected with the inauguration of the pope, but the palace is now uninhabited. It presents, however, in its ruins, a vast and imposing, though desolate aspect.

Lateranus was an unprincipled and dissolute man, and in consequence of certain crimes which he committed in connection with Messalina, during the reign of Claudius, he had been condemned to death. The sentence of death was not executed, though Lateranus was deprived of his rank, and doomed to live in retirement and disgrace. At the death of Claudius, and the accession of Nero, Lateranus was fully pardoned and restored to his former rank and position, through Nero's instrumentality. It might have been supposed that gratitude for these favors would have prevented Lateranus from joining such a conspiracy as this against his benefactor, but gratitude has very little place in the hearts of those who dwell in the courts and palaces of such tyrants as Nero.

The man on whom the conspirators relied most for efficient military aid, so far as such

aid should be needed in their enterprise, was
a certain Fenius Rufus, a captain of the imperial guards. He was a man of very resolute
and decided character, and was very highly
esteemed by the people of Rome. He was
not one of the originators of the plot, but
joined it at a later period; and when the
news of his accession to it was communicated
to the rest, it gave them great encouragement,
as they attached great importance to the ad
hesion of such a man to their cause. They
now immediately began to take measures for
executing their plans.

There was a woman in the secret of this
conspiracy, though how she obtained a knowledge of it no one seemed to know. Her name
was Epicharis. While the execution of the
plans of the confederates was delayed, Epicharis came to the principal conspirators
privately, first to one and then to another, and
urged them to action. None of the members
of the plot would admit that they had given
her any information on the subject, and how
she obtained her information no one could
tell. She was a woman of bad character, and
as such women often are, she was violent and
implacable in her hatred. She hated Nero,

and was so impatient at the delay of the conspirators that she made repeated and earnest
efforts to urge them on.

The conspirators in the mean time held
various secret meetings to mature their plans,
and to complete the preparation for the execution of them. They designed to destroy
Nero by some violent means, and then to
cause Piso to be proclaimed emperor in his
place. Piso was a man well suited for their
purpose in this respect. He was tall and
graceful in form, and his personal appearance
was in every respect prepossessing. His rank
was very high, and he was held in great estimation by all the people of the city for the
many generous and noble qualities that he
possessed. He was allied, too, to the most
illustrious families of Rome, and he occupied
in all respects so conspicuous a position, and
was so much an object of popular favor, that
the conspirators believed that his elevation to
the empire could easily be effected, if Nero
himself could once be put out of the way. To
effect the assassination of Nero, therefore, was
the first step.

After much debate, and many consultations
in respect to the best course to be pursued, it

was decided to accept the offer of a certain
Subrius Flavius, who undertook to kill the
emperor in the streets, at night, at some time
when he was roaming about in his carousals.
Flavius, in fact, was very daring and resolute
in his proposals, though wanting, as it proved
in the end, in the fulfillment of them. He
offered to stab Nero in the theater, when he
was singing on the stage, in the midst of all
the thousands of spectators convened there
This the conspirators thought, it seems, an un-
necessarily bold and desperate mode of accomplishing the end in view, and the plan
was accordingly overruled. Flavius then
proposed to set the palace on fire some night
when Nero was out in the city, and then, in
the confusion that would ensue, and while the
attention of the guards who had accompanied
Nero should be drawn toward the fire, to
assassinate the emperor in the streets. This
plan was acceded to by the conspirators, and
it was left to Flavius to select a favorable
time for the execution of it.

Time passed on, however, and nothing was
done. The favorable time which Flavius
looked for did not appear. In the mean-
while Epicharis became more and more im-

patient of the delay. She urged the conspirators to do their work, and chided in the
strongest terms their irresolution and pusil
.animity. At length finding that her invectives and reproaches were of no avail, she determined to leave them, and to see what she
could do herself toward the attainment of the
end.

She accordingly left Rome and proceeded
southwardly along the coast till she came to
Misenum, which, as has already been said,
was the great naval station of the empire at
this time. Epicharis went to some of the officers of the fleet, many of whom she knew,—
and in a very secret and cautious manner
made known to them the nature of the plot
which had been formed at Rome for the destruction of Nero and the elevation of Piso to
the empire in his stead. Before, however,
communicating intelligence of the conspiracy
to any persons whatever, Epicharis would converse with them secretly and confidentially
to learn how they were affected toward Nero
and his government. If she found them well
disposed she said nothing. If on the other
hand any one appeared discontented with the
government, or hostile to it in any way, she

would cautiously make known to him the
plans which were concocting at Rome for the
overthrow of it. She took care, however, in
these conversations to have never more than
one person present with her at a time, and
she revealed none of the names of the conspirators.

Among the other officers of the fleet was a
certain Proculus, who was one of the first with
whom Epicharis communicated. Proculus
was one of the men who had been employed
by Nero in his attempts to assassinate Agrippina his mother, and for his services on that
occasion had been promoted to the command
of a certain number of ships, a number containing in all one thousand men. This pro-
motion, however, as Epicharis found when she
came to converse with him, Proculus did not
consider as great a reward as his services had
deserved. The perpetration of so horrible a
crime as the murder of the emperor's mother,
merited, in his opinion, as he said to Epicharis, a much higher recompense than the command of a thousand men. Epicharis thought
so too. She talked with Proculus about his
wrongs, and the injuries which he suffered
from Nero's ingratitude and neglect, until she

fancied that he was in a state of mind which would prepare him to join in the plans of the conspirators, and then she cautiously unfolded them to him.

Proculus listened with great apparent interest to Epicharis's communication, and pretended to enter very cordially into the plan of the conspiracy; but as soon as the interview was ended he immediately left Misenum, and proceeded immediately to Rome, where he divulged the whole design to Nero.

Nero was exceedingly alarmed, and sent officers off at once to seize Epicharis and bring her before him. Epicharis, when questioned and confronted with Proculus, resolutely denied that she had ever held any such conversation with Proculus as he alledged, and feigned the utmost astonishment at what she termed the impudence of his accusation. She called for witnesses and proofs. Proculus of course could produce none, for Epicharis had taken care that there should be no third person present at their interviews. Proculus could not even give the names of any of the conspirators at Rome. He could only persist in his declaration that Epicharis had really disclosed to him the existence of the conspiracy, and had proposed to him to join in it; while she on the contrary as strenuously and positively denied it. Nero was perplexed. He found it impossible to determine what to believe. He finally dismissed Proculus, and sent Epicharis to prison, intending that she should remain there until he could make a more full examination into the case, and determine what to do.

In the mean time the conspirators became considerably alarmed when they heard of the arrest of Epicharis, and though they knew that thus far she had revealed nothing, they could not tell how soon her fidelity and firmness might yield under the tortures to which she was every day liable to be subjected; and as there appeared to be now no prospect that Flavius would ever undertake to execute his plan, they began to devise some other means of attaining the end.

It seems that Piso possessed at this time a villa and country-seat at Baiæ, on the coast south of Rome, and near to Misenum, and that Nero was accustomed sometimes to visit Piso here. It was now proposed by some of the conspirators that Piso should invite Nero to visit him at this villa, as if to witness some

spectacles or shows which should be arranged
for his entertainment there, and that then
persons employed for the purpose should sud
denly assassinate him, when off his guard, iɪ
the midst of some scene of convivial pleasure.
Piso, however, objected to this plan. He conceived, he said, that it would be dishonorable
in him to commit an act of violence upon a
guest whom he had invited under his roof, as
his friend. He was willing to take his full
share of the responsibility of destroying the
tyrant in any fair and manly way, but he
would not violate the sacred rites of hospital
ity to accomplish the end.

So this plan was abandoned. It was supposed, however, that Piso had another and a
deeper reason for his unwillingness that Nero
should be assassinated at Baiæ than his regard for his honor as a host. He thought, it
was said, that it would not be safe for him to
be away from Rome when the death of Nero
should be proclaimed in the capitol, lest some
other Roman nobleman or great officer of
state should suddenly arise in the emergency
and assume the empire. There were, in fact,
one or two men in Rome of great power and
influence, of whom Piso was specially jealous

and he was naturally very much disposed to
be on his guard against opening any door of
pportunity for them to rise to power. To
commit a great crime in order to secure his own
aggrandizement, and yet to manage the commission of it in such a way as not only to shut
himself off from the expected benefit, but to
secure that benefit to a hated rival, would
have been a very fatal misstep. So the plan
of destroying Nero at Baiæ was overruled.

At length one more, and as it proved a final
scheme, was formed for accomplishing the
purpose of the conspiracy. It was determined
to execute Nero in Rome, at a great public
celebration which was then about to take
place. It seems that it was sometimes customary in ancient times for persons who had
any request or petition to make to an emperor or king, to avail themselves of the occasion of such celebrations to present them.
Accordingly it was determined that Lateranus
should approach Nero at a certain time during the celebration of the games, as if to
offer a petition,—the other conspirators being
close at hand, and ready to act at a moment's
warning. Lateranus, as soon as he was near
enough, was to kneel down and suddenly

Nero to be slain in the theatre.

draw the emperor's robes about his feet, and then clasp the feet thus enveloped, in his arms, so as to render Nero helpless. The other conspirators were then to rush forward and kill their victim with their daggers. In the mean time while Lateranus and his associates were perpetrating this deed in the circus where the games were to be exhibited, Piso was to station himself in a certain temple not far distant, to await the result; while Fenius, the officer of the guard, who has already been mentioned as the chief military reliance of the conspirators, was to be posted in another part of the city, with a military cavalcade in array, ready to proceed through the streets and bring Piso forth to be proclaimed emperor as soon as he should receive the tidings that Nero had been slain. It is said that in order to give additional éclat and popularity to the proceeding, it was arranged that Octavia, a daughter of Claudius, the former emperor, was to be brought forward with Piso in the cavalcade, as if to combine the influence of her hereditary claims, whatever they might be, with the personal popularity of Piso in favor of the new government about to be established.

15—16

Thus every thing was arranged. To each
conspirator, his own particular duty was assigned, and, as the day approached for the
execution of the scheme, every thing seemed
to promise success. It is obvious, however,
that, as the affair had been arranged, all
would depend upon the resolution and fidel
ity of those who had been designated to stab
the emperor with their daggers, when Lateranus should have grasped his feet. The
slightest faltering or fear at this point, would
be fatal to the whole scheme. The man on
whom the conspirators chiefly relied for this
part of their work, was a certain desperate
profligate, named Scevinus, who had been
one of the earliest originators of the conspiracy, and one of the most dauntless and determined of the promoters of it, so far as words
and professions could go. He particularly
desired that the privilege of plunging the
first dagger into Nero's heart should be
granted to him. He had a knife, he said,
which he had found in a certain temple a long
time before, and which he had preserved and
carried about his person constantly ever since,
for some such deed. So it was arranged that
Scevinus should strike the fatal blow.

As the time drew nigh, Scevinus seemed
to grow more and more excited with the
thoughts of what was before him. He attracted the attention of the domestics at his
house, by his strange and mysterious demean-
or. He held a long and secret consultation
with Natalis, another conspirator, on the
day before the one appointed for the execution of the plot, under such circumstances as
to increase still more the wonder and curios
ity of his servants. He formally executed
his will, as if he were approaching some dangerous crisis. He made presents to his servants, and actually emancipated one or two
of his favorite slaves. He talked with all he
met, in a rapid and incoherent manner, on
various subjects, and with an air of gayety
and cheerfulness which it was obvious to
those who observed him was all assumed;
for, in the intervals of these conversations,
and at every pause, he relapsed into a
thoughtful and absent mood, as if he were
meditating some deep and dangerous design.

That night, too, he took out his knife from
its sheath, and gave it to one of his servants,
named Milichus, to be ground. He directed
Milichus to be particularly attentive to the

He gives his knife to Milichus to be ground.

THE KNIFE.

sharpening of the point. Before Milichus
brought back the knife, Scevinus directed
him to prepare bandages such as would be
suitable for binding up wounds to stop the
effusion of blood. Milichus observed all these
directions, and, having made all the preparations required, according to the orders which
Scevinus had given him — keeping the knife,
however, still in his possession — he went to
report the whole case to his wife, in order to

consult with her in respect to the meaning of all these mysterious indications.

The wife of Milichus soon came to the conclusion, that these strange proceedings could denote nothing less than a plot against the life of the emperor; and she urged her husband to go early the next morning, and make known his discovery. She told him that it was impossible that such a conspiracy should succeed, for it must be known to a great many persons, some one of whom would be sure to divulge it in hope of a reward. "If you divulge it," she added, "you will secure the reward for yourself; and if you do not, you will be supposed to be privy to it, when it is made known by others, and so will be sacrificed with the rest to Nero's anger."

Milichus was convinced by his wife's reasonings, and on the following morning, as soon as the day dawned, he rose and repaired to the palace. At first he was refused admittance, but on sending word to the officer of the household, that he had intelligence of the most urgent importance to communicate to Nero, they allowed him to come in. When brought into Nero's presence, he told his story, describing particularly all the circum

16

stances that he had observed, which had led
him to suppose that a conspiracy was formed.
He spoke of the long and mysterious consultation which Scevinus and Natalis had held
together on the preceding day; he described
the singular conduct and demeanor which
Scevinus had subsequently manifested, the
execution of his will, his wild and incoherent
conversation, his directions in respect to the
sharpening of the knife and the preparation
of the bandages; and, to crown his proofs, he
produced the knife itself, which he had kept
for this purpose, and which thus furnished, in
some sense, an ocular demonstration of the
truth of what he had declared.

Officers were immediately sent to seize
Scevinus, and to bring him into the presence
of the emperor. Scevinus knew, of course,
that the only possible hope for him was in a
bold and resolute denial of the charge made
against him. He accordingly denied, in the
most solemn manner, that there was any plot
or conspiracy whatever, and he attempted to
explain all the circumstances which had
awakened his servant's suspicions. The knife
or dagger which Milichus had produced, was
an ancient family relic, he said,—one which

he had kept for a long time in his chamber, and which his servant had obtained surreptitiously, for the purpose of sustaining his false and malicious charge against his master. As to his will, he often made and signed a will anew, he said, as many other persons were accustomed to do, and no just inference against him could be drawn from the circumstance that he had done this on the preceding day ; and in respect to the bandages and other preparation for the dressing of wounds which Milichus alledged that he had ordered, he denied the statement altogether. He had not given any such orders. The whole story was the fabrication of a vile slave, attempting, by these infamous means, to compass his master's destruction. Scevinus said all this with so bold and intrepid a tone of voice, and with such an air of injured innocence, that Nero and his friends were half disposed to believe that he was unjustly accused, and to dismiss him from custody. This might very probably have been the result, and Milichus himself might have been punished for making a false and malicious accusation, had not the sagacity of his wife, who was all the time watching these proceedings with the most anxious interest, furnished a clew which, in the end, brought the whole truth to light.

She called attention to the long conference which Scevinus had held with Natalis on the preceding day. Scevinus was accordingly questioned concerning it. He declared that his interview was nothing but an innocent consultation about his own private affairs. He was questioned then about the particulars of the conversation. Of course he was compelled to fabricate a statement in reply. Natalis himself was then sent for, and examined, apart from Scevinus, in regard to the conversation they had held together. Natalis, of course, fabricated a story too,—but, as usual with such fabrications, the two accounts having been invented independently, were inconsistent with each other. Nero was immediately convinced that the men were guilty, and that some sort of plot or conspiracy had been formed. He ordered that they should both be put to the torture in order to compel them to confess their crime, and disclose the names of their accomplices. In the mean time they were sent to prison, and loaded with irons, to be kept in that condition until the instruments of torture could be prepared.

When at length they were brought to the rack, the sight of the horrid machinery unmanned them. They begged to be spared, and promised to reveal the whole. They acknowledged that a conspiracy had been formed, and gave the names of all who had participated in it. They explained fully, too, the plans which had been devised, and as in this case, though they were examined separately, their statements agreed, Nero and his friends were convinced of the truth of their declarations, and thus at last the plot was fully brought to light. Nero himself was struck with consternation and terror at discovering the formidable danger to which he had been exposed.

Chapter XI.

The Fate of the Conspirators.

AS soon as Nero had obtained all the information which he and his officers could draw from Scevinus and Natalis, and had sent to all parts of the city to arrest those whom the forced disclosures of these witnesses accused, he thought of Epicharis, who, it will be recollected, had been sent to prison, and who was still in confinement there. He ordered Epicharis to be told that concealment was no longer possible,—that Scevinus and Natalis had divulged the plot in full, and that her only hope lay in amply confessing all that she knew.

This announcement had no effect upon Epicharis. She refused to admit that she knew any thing of any conspiracy.

Nero then ordered that she should be put to the torture. The engines were prepared and she was brought before them. The sight of them produced no change. She was then placed upon the wheel, and her frail and delicate limbs were stretched, dislocated, and broken, until she had endured every form of agony which such engines could produce Her constancy remained unshaken to the end. At length, when she was so much exhausted by her sufferings that she could no longer feel the pain, she was taken away to be restored by medicaments, cordials, and rest, in order that she might recover strength to endure new tortures on the following day.

In the mean time, panic and excitement reigned throughout the city. Nero doubled his guards; he garrisoned his palace; he brought out bodies of armed men, and stationed them on the walls of the city and in the public squares, or marched them to and fro about the streets. As fast as men were accused they were put to the question, and as each one saw that the only hope for safety to himself was in freely denouncing others, the names of supposed confederates were revealed in great numbers, and as fast as these names were obtained the men were seized and imprisoned or executed—the innocent and the guilty together.

On the very first announcement that the plot had been discovered, those of the con-

spirators who were still at large made all
haste to the house of Piso. They found him
prostrate in consternation and despair. They
urged him immediately to come forth, and to
put himself at the head of an armed force,
and fight for his life. Desperate as such an
undertaking might be, no other alternative,
they said, was now left to him. But all was
of no avail. The conspirators could not arouse
him to action. They were obliged to retire
and leave him to his fate. He opened the
veins in his arm, and bled to death while the
soldiers whom Nero had sent were breaking
into his house to arrest him.

Being thus deprived of their leader, the
conspirators gave up all hope of effecting the
revolution, and thought only of the means of
screening themselves from Nero's vengeance.

In the mean time, Epicharis had so far recovered during the night, that on the following morning it was determined to bring her
again to the torture. She was utterly helpless,—her limbs having been broken by the
execution of the day before. The officers accordingly put her into a sort of sedan chair, or
covered litter, in order that she might be carried by bearers to the place of torture. She was

BRINGING EPICHARIS TO THE TORTURE.

borne in this way to the spot, but when the
executioners opened the door of the chair to
take her out, they beheld a shocking spectacle.
Their wretched victim had escaped from their
power. She was hanging by the neck, dead.
She had contrived to make a noose in one end
of the cincture with which she was girded, and
fastening the other end to some part of the
chair within, she had succeeded in bringing
the weight of her body upon the noose around

her neck, and had died without disturbing her bearers as they walked along.

In the mean time the various parties that were accused were seized in great numbers, nd were brought in for trial before a sort of court-martial which Nero himself, with some of his principal officers, held for this purpose in the gardens of the palace. The number of those accused was so large that the avenues to the garden were blocked up with them, and with the parties of soldiers that conducted them, and multitudes were detained together at the gates, in a state, of course, of awful suspense and agitation, waiting their turns. It happened singularly enough that among those whom Nero summoned to serve on the tribunal for the trial of the prisoners were two of the principal conspirators, who had not yet been accused. These were Subrius Flavius and Fenius Rufus, whom the reader will perhaps recollect as prominent members of the plot. Flavius was the man who had once undertaken to kill the emperor in the streets, and while standing near him at the tribunal, he made signs to the other conspirators that he was ready to stab him to the heart now, if they would but say the word. But Rufus

restrained him, anxiously signifying to him
that he was by no means to attempt it. Rufus
in fact seems to have been as weak-minded
and irresolute as Flavius was desperate and
bold.

In fact although Rufus, when summoned to
attend in the garden, for the trial of the conspirators, did not dare to disobey, he yet found
it very difficult to summon resolution to face
the appalling dangers of his position. He
took his place at last among the others, and
with a forced external composure which ill
concealed the desperate agitation and anxiety
which reigned in his soul, he gave himself to
the work of trying and condemning his confederates and companions. For a time no
one of them betrayed him. But at length during the examination of Scevinus, in his solicitude to appear zealous in Nero's cause he
overacted his part, so far as to press Scevinus
too earnestly with his inquiries, until at
length Scevinus turned indignantly toward
him saying—

"Why do *you* ask these questions? No
person in Rome knows more about this conspiracy than you, and if you feel so devoted
to this humane and virtuous prince of yours,

show your gratitude by telling him, yourself, the whole story."

Rufus was perfectly overwhelmed at this sudden charge, and could not say a word. He attempted to speak, but he faltered and stammered, and then sank down into his seat, pale and trembling, and covered with confusion. Nero and the other members of the tribunal were convinced of his guilt. He was seized and put in irons, and after the same summary trial to which the rest were subjected, condemned to die. He begged for his life with the most earnest and piteous lamentations, but Nero was relentless, and he was immediately beheaded.

The conspirator Flavius displayed a very different temper. When he came to be accused, at first he denied the charge, and he appealed to his whole past character and course of life as proof of his innocence. Those who had informed against him, however, soon furnished incontestable evidence of his guilt, and then changing his ground, he openly acknowledged his share in the conspiracy and gloried in it even in the presence of Nero himself. When Nero asked him how he could so violate his oath of allegiance and fidelity as to conspire against the life of his sovereign, he turned to him with looks of open and angry defiance and said—

"It was because I hated and detested you, unnatural monster as you are. There was a time when there was not a soldier in your service who was more devoted to you than I. But that time has passed. You have drawn upon yourself the detestation and abhorrence of all mankind by your cruelties and your crimes. You have murdered your mother. You have murdered your wife. You are an incendiary. And not content with perpetrating these enormous atrocities, you have degraded yourself in the eyes of all Rome to the level of the lowest mountebank and buffoon, so as to make yourself the object of contempt as well as abhorrence. I hate and defy you."

Nero was of course astonished and almost confounded at hearing such words. He had never listened to language like this before. His astonishment was succeeded by violent rage, and he ordered Flavius to be led out to immediate execution.

The centurion to whom the execution was committed conducted Flavius without the city to a field, and then set the soldiers at work to

15—17

dig the grave, as was customary at military
executions, while he made the other necessary
preparations. The soldiers, in their haste,
shaped the excavation rudely and imperfectly.
Flavius ridiculed their work, asking them, in
a tone of contempt, if they considered that the
proper way to dig a military grave. And
when at length, after all the preparations had
been made, and the fatal moment had arrived, the tribune who was in command called
upon him to uncover his neck and stand forth
courageously to meet his fate—he replied by
exhorting the officer himself to be resolute
and firm. "See," said he, "if you can show
as much nerve in striking the blow, as I can
in meeting it." To cut down such a man,
under such circumstances, was of course a
very dreadful duty, even for a Roman soldier, and the executioner faltered greatly in
the performance of it. The decapitation
should have been effected by a single blow;
but the officer found his strength failing him
when he came to strike, so that a second blow
was necessary to complete the severance of
the head from the body. The tribune was
afraid that this, when represented to Nero,
might bring him under suspicion, as if it in

dicated some shrinking on his part from a prompt and vigorous action in putting down the conspiracy; and so on his return to Nero he boasted of his performance as if it had been just as he intended. "I made the trai tor die twice," said he, "by taking two blows to dispatch him."

But perhaps the most melancholy of all the results of this most unfortunate conspiracy, was the fate of Seneca. Seneca, it will be remembered, had been Nero's instructor and guardian in former years, and subsequently one of his chief ministers of state. He was now almost seventy years of age, and besides the veneration in which he was held on this account, and the respect that was paid to the exalted position which he had occupied for so long a period, he was very highly esteemed for his intellectual endowments and for his private character. His numerous writings, in fact, had acquired for him an extensive literary fame.

But Nero hated him. He had long wished him out of the way. It was currently reported, and generally believed, that he had attempted to poison him. However this may be, he certainly desired to find some occasion of proceeding against him, and such an occasion was furnished by the developments connected with this conspiracy.

Natalis, in the course of his testimony, said that he supposed that Seneca was concerned in the plot, for he recollected that he was once sent to him, while he was confined to his house by illness, with a message from Piso. The message was, that Piso had repeatedly called at his, that is, Seneca's house, but had been unable to obtain admittance. The answer which Seneca had returned was, that the reason why he had not received visitors was, that the state of his health was very infirm, but that he entertained none but friendly feelings toward Piso, and wished him prosperity and success.

Nero determined to consider this as proof that Seneca was privy to the conspiracy, and that he secretly abetted it. At least he determined, for a first step, to send an officer with a band of armed men to arrest him, and to lay the crime to his charge. Seneca was not in the city at this time. He had been absent in Campania, which was a beautiful rural region, south of Rome, back from Misenum. He was, however, that very day on his return to Rome, and Silvanus, the officer whom Nero sent to him, met him on the way, at a villa which he possessed a few miles from Rome. The name of this villa was Nomentanum.* Seneca had stopped at the villa to spend the night, and was seated at the table with Paulina his wife, when Silvanus and his troop arrived.

The soldiers surrounded the house, so as to prevent all possibility of escape, and posted sentinels at the doors. Silvanus and some of his associates then went in, and entering the hall where Seneca was at supper, they informed him for what purpose they were come. Silvanus repeated what Natalis had testified in respect to the messages which had passed between Seneca and Piso. Seneca admitted that the statement was true, but he declared that the word which he had sent to Piso was only an ordinary message of civility and friendliness; it meant nothing more. Finding that no farther explanation could be obtained, Silvanus left Seneca in his villa, with a strong guard posted around the house, and returned to Rome to report to Nero.

When Nero had heard the report, he asked

* See map. Frontispiece.

17

Silvanus whether Seneca appeared sufficiently terrified by the accusation to make it probable that he would destroy himself that night.* Silvanus answered no. "He displayed," said he, "no marks of fear. There was no agitation, no sign of regret, no token of sorrow. His words and looks bespoke a mind calm, confident and firm."

"Go to him," rejoined Nero, "and tell him that he must make up his mind to die."

Silvanus was thunderstruck at receiving this order. He could not believe it possible that Nero would really put to death a man so venerable in years and wisdom, who had been to him all his life, in the place of a father. Instead of proceeding directly to Seneca's house he went to consult with the captain of the guard, who, though really one of the conspirators, had not yet been accused, and was still at liberty, though trembling with appre-

* It seems to have been considered by public men in those days, that to resolve on self-destruction was a much more honorable course to pursue in an extreme emergency like this, than to wait to be condemned and executed by the officers of the law. The attempt to frighten a man into the act of killing himself was accordingly *one* of the various modes which a tyrant might resort to, to remove those who were obnoxious to him.

hension at the imminence of his danger. The
captain, after hearing the case, said that
nothing was to be done but to deliver the
message. Silvanus then went to Seneca's
villa, but not being able to endure the thought
of being himself the bearer of such tidings,
sent in a centurion with the message.

Seneca received it with calm composure,
and immediately made preparations for ter
minating his life. His wife Paulina insisted
on sharing his fate. He gathered his friends
around him to give them his parting counsels
and bid them farewell, and ordered his servants to make the necessary preparations for
opening his veins. Then ensued one of those
sad and awful scenes of mourning and death,
with which the page of ancient history is so
often darkened—forming pictures, as they do,
too shocking to be exhibited in full detail.
The calm composure of Seneca, was con-
trasted on the one hand with the bitter anguish and loud lamentations of his domestics
and friends, and on the other with Paulina's
mute despair. When the veins were opened,
the blood at first would not flow, and various
artificial means were resorted to, to accelerate
the extinction of life; at last, however, Sen-

eca ceased to breathe. The domestics of the
family then begged and entreated the soldiers
with many tears, that they might be allowed
to save Paulina if it were not too late. The
soldiers consented; so the women bound up
her wounds, as she lay insensible and helpless before them, and thus stopping the farther effusion of blood, they watched over her
with assiduous care, in hopes to restore her.
They succeeded. They brought her back to
life, or rather to a semblance of life; for she
never really recovered so as to be herself
again, during the few lonely and desolate
years through which she afterward lingered.

There was another Roman citizen of the
highest rank who fell an innocent victim to
the angry passions which the discovery of
this plot awakened in Nero's mind. It was
the consul Vestinus. Vestinus was a man
of great loftiness of character, and had never
evinced that pliancy of temper, and that sub-
missiveness to the imperial will, which Nero
required. His position, too, as consul, which
was the highest civil office in the commonwealth, gave him a vast influence over the
people of Rome, so that Nero feared as well
as hated him. In fact, so great was his in

dependence of character, and his intractability, as it was sometimes called, that the conspirators, after mature deliberation, had concluded not to propose to him to engage in the plot. But, though he was thus innocent, Nero did not certainly know the fact, and, at any rate, such an opportunity to effect the destruction of a hated rival, was too good to be lost. Very soon, therefore, after the disclosure of the conspiracy had been made, Nero sent a tribune, at the head of five hundred men, to arrest the consul.

This large force was designated for the service, partly because,—on account of the high rank and office of the accused,—Nero did not know what means of resistance the consul might be able to command, and partly because his house, which was situated in the most public part of the city, overlooking the Forum, was in itself a sort of citadel, of which the various officers of Vestinus's household, and his numerous retainers, constituted a sort of garrison. It happened that, at the time when Nero sent his troop to make the arrest, Vestinus was entertaining a large party of friends at supper. The festivities were suddenly interrupted, and the whole company were thrown into a state of the most frightful excitement and confusion, by the sudden onset of this large body of armed men, who besieged the doors, blocked up all the avenues of approach, and, surrounding and guarding the house on every side, shut all the inmates in, as if they were investing the castle of an enemy. Certain soldiers of the guard were then sent in to Vestinus in the banqueting-room, to inform him that the tribune wished to speak with him on important business.

The consul knew the character of Nero, and the feelings which the tyrant entertained toward him too well, and saw too clearly the advantage which the discovery of the conspiracy gave to Nero, not to perceive at once that his fate was sealed; and the action which he took in this frightful emergency comported well with his insubmissive and intractable character. Instead of obeying the summons of the tribune, he repaired immediately to a private apartment, summoned his physician, directed a bath to be prepared, ordered the physician to open his veins, lay down in the bath to promote the flowing of the blood, and in a few minutes ceased to breathe.

The announcement of the consul s death, when it came to be reported to Nero, of course gave him great satisfaction. He continued the guards, however, still about the house, keeping the guests imprisoned in the banqueting-room for many hours. Of course, during all this time, the minds of these guests were in a state of extreme distress and apprehension, inasmuch as every one of them must necessarily have felt in immediate danger. When the anxiety and agitation which they felt, was reported to Nero, he was greatly entertained by it, and said that they were paying for their consular supper. He kept them in this state of suspense until nearly morning, and then ordered the guards to be withdrawn.

The number of victims who were sacrificed to Nero's resentment in consequence of this conspiracy, was very large; so that the streets were filled with executions and with funeral processions for many days. Universal grief and panic prevailed, and yet no one dared to manifest the slightest indications of sorrow or of fear. The people supposed that pity for the sufferers, or anxiety for themselves, would be interpreted as proofs that they had been concerned in the conspiracy; for multitudes of those who had been put to death, were condemned on pretexts and pretended proofs of the most frivolous character. Every one, therefore, even of those whose nearest and dearest friends had been killed, was compelled to assume all the appearances of extravagant joy that so wicked a plot against the life of so wise and excellent a prince, had been exposed, and the guilty devisers of it brought to punishment. Parents whose sons had been slain, and wives and children who had lost their husbands and fathers, were thus compelled to unite in the congratulations and expressions of joy which were everywhere addressed to the emperor. Processions were formed, addresses were made, sacrifices were offered, games, spectacles, and illuminations without number were celebrated, to testify to the general rejoicing; and thus the city presented all the outward appearances of universal gladness and joy, while, in truth, the hearts of men were everywhere overwhelmed with anxiety, grief, and fear.

When at length a sufficient number of the citizens of Rome had been destroyed, Nero assembled the army, and after making an address to the troops on the subject of the conspiracy, and on his happy escape from the danger, he divided an immense sum of money from the public treasury among the soldiers, so as to give a very considerable largess to each man. He also distributed among them a vast amount of provisions from the public granaries. This act, and the connection between Nero and the troops which it illustrates, explain what would otherwise seem an inscrutable mystery, namely, how it can be possible for one man to bring the immense population of such an empire as that of ancient Rome so entirely under his power, that any number of the most prominent and influential of the citizens shall be siezed and beheaded, or thrust through the heart with swords and daggers at a word or a nod from him. The explanation is, *the army*. Give to the single tyrant one or two hundred thousand desperadoes, well banded together, and completely armed, under a compact between them by which he says, "Help me to control, to domineer over, and to plunder the industrial classes of society, and I will give you a large share of the spoil," and the work is very easy. The governments that have existed in the

world have generally been formed on this
plan. They have been simply vast armies
authorized to collect their own pay by the
systematic plunder of the millions whose
peaceful industry feeds and clothes the world.
The remedy which mankind is now beginning
to discover and apply is equally simple. The
millions who do the work are learning to keep
the arms in their own hands, and to forbid
the banding together of masses of troops for
the purpose of exalting pride and cruelty to
a position of absolute and irresponsible power.

In Nero's case, so great was the awe which
the terrible power of the Roman legions inspired, that even the Senate bowed humbly
before it, and joined in the general adulation
of the hated tyrant. They decreed oblations
and public thanksgivings; they erected new
temples to express their gratitude to the gods
for so signal a deliverance; they instituted
new games and festivities to express the general joy, and erected statues and monuments
in honor of those who had contributed to the
discovery of the plot. The knife or dagger
which Milichus had produced as the one by
which Nero was to have been slain, was preserved as a sacred relic. A suitable inscrip-

tion was placed upon it, and it was deposited, with all solemnity, in one of the temples of the city, there to remain a memorial of the event for all future generations. In a word, the tyrant's escape from death called forth all the outward manifestations of joy which could have been deserved by the greatest public benefactor.

And yet, notwithstanding all this, such was the estimate which public sentiment really entertained of the true character of Nero, that it was considered extremely doubtful at the time, and has, in fact, been so considered ever since, whether there ever was any conspiracy at all. It was very extensively believed that the whole pretended discovery of the plot was an ingenious device on the part of Nero, to furnish him with plausible pretexts for destroying a great number of men who were personally obnoxious to him. And were it not almost impossible to believe that such monstrous wickedness and tyranny as that of Nero could riot so long over Romans without arousing them to some desperate attempts to destroy him, we might ourselves adopt this view, and suppose that this celebrated plot was wholly a fabrication.

CHAPTER XII.

THE EXPEDITION INTO GREECE.

AS the excitement which had been produced by the discovery, real or pretended, of Piso's conspiracy, and by the innumerable executions which were attendant
upon it, passed away, Nero returned to his
usual mode of life, and in fact abandoned
himself to the indulgence of his brutal propensities and passions more recklessly than
ever. He spent his days in sloth, and his
nights in rioting and carousals, and was rapidly becoming an object of general contempt
and detestation. The only ambition which
seemed to animate him was to excel, or rather
to have the credit of excelling, as a player
and singer on the public stage.

Not long after the period of the conspiracy
described in the last two chapters, and when
the excitement connected with it had in some
measure subsided, the attention of the public
began to be turned toward a great festival, the
time for which was then approaching. This

festival was celebrated with spectacles and
games of various kinds, which were called
the quinquennial games, from the circumstance that the period for the celebration of
them recurred once in five years. A princi
pal part of the performances on these occasions consisted of contests for prizes, which
were offered for those who chose to compete
for them. Some of these prizes were for those
who excelled in athletic exercises, and in
feats of strength and dexterity, while others
were for singers and dancers, and other performers on the public stage. Nero could not
resist the temptation to avail himself of this
grand occasion for the display of his powers,
and he prepared to appear among the other
actors and mountebanks as a competitor for
the theatrical prizes.

Performers on the public stage were regarded in ancient days much as they are
now. They were applauded, flattered, caressed, and most extravagantly paid; but
after all they formed a social class distinct
from all others, and of a very low grade.
Just as now great public singers are rewarded
sometimes with the most princely revenues,—
not twice or three times, but *ten* times per-

15—18

haps the amount ever paid to the highest ministers of state,—and receive the most flattering attentions from the highest classes of society, and are followed by crowds in the public streets, and enter cities escorted by grand processions, while yet there is scarce a respectable citizen of the better class who would not feel himself demeaned at seeing his son or his daughter on the stage by their side.

In the same manner public sentiment was such in the city of Rome, in Nero's day, that to see the chief military magistrate of the commonwealth publicly performing on the stage, and entering into an eager competition with the singing men and women, the low comedians, the dancers, the buffoons, and other such characters, that figured there, was a very humiliating spectacle. In fact, when the time for the quinquennial celebration approached, the government attempted to prevent the necessity of the emperor's actual appearing upon the stage, by passing in the Senate, among other decrees relating to the celebrations, certain votes awarding honorary crowns and prizes to Nero, by anticipation,— thus acknowledging him to be the first with out requiring the test of actual competition. But this did not satisfy Nero. In fact, the honor of being publicly proclaimed victor was not probably the chief allurement which attracted him. He wished to enjoy the excitement and the pleasure of the contest,—to see the vast audience assembled before him, and held in charmed and enraptured attention by his performance ; and to listen to and enjoy the triumphant grandeur of the applause which rolled and reverberated in the great Roman amphitheaters on such occasions with the sound of thunder. In a word it was the vanity of personal display, rather than ambition for an honorable distinction, that constituted the motive which actuated him.

He consequently disregarded the honorary awards which the Senate had decreed him, and insisted on actually appearing on the stage. His first performance was the reciting of a poem which he had composed. The poem was received, of course, with unbounded applause. Afterward he appeared on the stage in competition with the harpers and other musical performers. The populace applauded his efforts with the greatest enthusiasm, while the more respectable citizens were silent, or spoke to each other in secret murmurs of discontent and disapproval. There were a great many rules and restrictions which the candidates in these contests were required to observe; and though they were all proper enough for the class of men for whom they were intended, were yet such that the emperor, in subjecting himself to them, placed himself in a very low and degraded position, so as to become an object of ridicule and contempt. For example, after coming to the end of a performance on the harp, he would advance to the front of the stage, and there, after the manner customary among the players of that day, would kneel down in an imploring attitude, with his hands raised, as if humbly soliciting a favorable sentence from the audience, as his judges, and tremblingly waiting their decision. This, considering that the suppliant performer was the greatest potentate on earth, officially responsible for the government of half the world, and the audience before whom he was kneeling was mainly composed of the lowest rabble of the city, seemed to every respectable Roman, absurd and ridiculous to the last degree.

Nevertheless, the fame of these exploits

performed by Nero as a public actor, spread
gradually throughout the empire, and the
subject attracted special attention in the cities
of Greece, where games and public spectacles
of every kind were celebrated with the greatest pomp and splendor.   Several of these
cities sent deputations to Rome, with crowns
and garlands for the emperor, which they had
decreed to him in honor of the skill and superiority which he had displayed in the his-
trionic art.   Nero was extremely gratified at
having such honors conferred upon him.   He
received the deputations which brought these
tokens, with great pomp and parade, as if they
had been embassadors from sovereign princes
or states, sent to transact business of the most
momentous concern.   He gave them audience,
in fact, before all others, and entertained
them with feasts and spectacles, and conferred
upon them every other mark of public consideration and honor.   On one occasion, at a
feast to which he had invited such a company
of embassadors, one of them asked him to favor them with a song.   The emperor at once
complied, and sang a song for the entertain
ment of the company at the table.   He was
rapturously applauded, and was so delighted
18

with the enthusiasm which his performance awakened, as to exclaim that the Greeks were, after all, the only people that really had a taste for music ; none but they, he said, could understand or appreciate a good song.

The most renowned of all the celebrations of the ancient Greeks were the Olympic games. These games constituted a grand national festival, which was held once in four years on a plain in the western part of the Peloponnesus, called the Olympian Plain. This plain was but little more than a mile in extent, and was bordered on one side by rocky hills, and on the other by the waters of a river. Here suitable structures were erected for the exhibition of the spectacles and games, and for the accommodation of the spectators, and when the period for the celebrations arrived, immense multitudes assembled from every part of Greece to witness the solemnities. The spectators, however, were all men; for with the exception of a few priestesses who had certain official duties to perform, no females were allowed to be present. The punishment for an attempt to evade this law was death ; for if any woman attempted to witness the scene in disguise, the law was that she was to be seized, if detected, and hurled down a neighboring precipice, to be killed by the fall. It is said, however, that only one case of such detection ever occurred, and in that case the woman was pardoned in consideration of the fact that her father, her brothers, and her son had all been victors in the games.

The games continued for five days. The general arrangements were made, and the umpires were appointed, by the government of Elis, which was the state in which the Olympian plain was situated. There was a gymnasium in the vicinity, where those who intended to enter the lists as competitors were accustomed to put themselves in training. This training occupied nearly a year, and for thirty days previous to the public exhibition the exercises were conducted at this gymnasium in the same manner and form as at the games themselves. There was a large and regularly organized police provided to preserve order, and umpires appointed with great formality, to decide the contests and make the awards. These umpires were inducted into office by the most solemn oaths. They bound themselves by these oaths to give just and true decisions without fear or favor.

The festival was opened, when the time
arrived, in the evening, by the offering of sacrifices,—the services being conducted in the
most imposing and solemn manner. On the
following morning at daybreak the games
and contests began. These consisted of races
—in chariots, on horseback, and on foot,—the
runners being in the latter case sometimes
dressed lightly, and sometimes loaded with
heavy armor;—of matches in leaping, wrest-
ling, boxing, and throwing the discus;—and
finally, of musical and poetical performances
of various kinds. To obtain the prize in any
of these contests was considered throughout
the whole Grecian world as an honor of the
highest degree.

The period for the celebration of these
games began to draw nigh, as it happened,
not long after the time when the deputations
from Greece came to Nero with the compli-
ments and crowns decreed to him in token of
their admiration of his public performances at
Rome,—and it is not at all surprising that his
attention and interest were strongly awakened
by the approach of so renowned a festival.
In short he resolved to go to Greece, and display his powers before the immense and dis-

tinguished audiences that were to assemble on the Olympic plains.

He accordingly organized a very large retinue of attendants and followers, and prepared to set out on his journey. This retinue was in numbers quite an army; but in character it was a mere troop of actors, musicians and buffoons. It was made up almost wholly of people connected in various ways with the stage, so that the baggage which followed in its train, instead of being formed of arms and munitions of war, as was usual when a great Roman commander had occasion to pass out of Italy, consisted of harps, fiddles, masks, buskins, and such other stage property as was in use in those times,—while the company itself was formed almost entirely of comedians, singers, dancers, and wrestlers, with an immense retinue of gay and dissipated men and women, who exemplified every possible stage of moral debasement and degradation. With this company Nero crossed to the eastern shore of Italy, and there, embarking on board the vessels which had been prepared for the voyage, he sailed over the Adriatic sea to the shores of Greece.

He landed at Cassiope, a town in the north-

ern part of the island of Corcyra. Here there
was a temple to Jupiter, and the first of Nero's
exploits was to go there and sing, being impatient, it would seem, to give the people of
Greece a specimen of his powers immediately
on landing. After this he passed over to the
continent, and thence advanced into the heart
of Greece, playing, singing, and acting in all
the cities through which he passed. As there
were yet some months to elapse before the period for celebrating the Olympic games, Nero
had ample time for making this tour. He was
of course everywhere received with the most
unbounded applause, for of course those only,
in general, who were most pleased with such
amusements, and were most inclined to ap-
prove of Nero's exhibiting himself as a performer, came together in the assemblies which
convened to hear him. Thus it happened that
the virtuous, the cultivated, and the refined,
remained at their homes; while all the idle,
reckless, and dissolute spirits of the land
flocked in crowds to the entertainments which
their imperial visitor offered them. These
men, of course, considered it quite a triumph
for them that so distinguished a potentate
should take an active part in ministering to

their pleasures; and thus wherever Nero went he was sure to be attended by crowds, and his performances, whether skillful or not, could not fail of being extravagantly extolled in conversation, and of eliciting in the theaters thunders of applause. The consequence was that Nero was delighted with the enthusiasm which his performances seemed everywhere to awaken. To be thus received and thus applauded in the cities of Greece, seemed to satisfy his highest ambition.

It has always been considered a very extra ordinary proof of mental and moral degrada- tion on the part of Nero, that he could thus descend from the exalted sphere of responsi- bility and duty to which his high official sta- tion properly consigned him, in order to min- gle in such scenes and engage in such contests as were exhibited in the ordinary theaters and circuses in Greece. It is however not so sur- prising that he should have been willing to appear as a competitor at the Olympic games : so prominent were these games above all the other athletic and military celebrations of that age, and so great was the value attached to the honor of a victory obtained in them. There was, it is true, no value in the prize itself, that was bestowed upon the victors. There was no silver cup, or golden crown, or sum of money staked upon the issue. The only direct award was a crown of olive leaves, which, at the close of the contest, was placed upon the head of the victor. Everything pertaining to this crown was connected with the most imposing and peculiar ceremonies. The leaves from which the garland was made were obtained from a certain sacred olive-tree, which grew in a consecrated grove in Olympia. The tree itself had been originally brought, it was said, from the country of the Hyperboreans, by Hercules, and planted in Olympia, where it was sacredly preserved to furnish garlands for the victors in the games. The leaves were cut from the tree by a boy chosen for the purpose. He gathered the leaves by means of a golden sickle, which was set apart expressly to this use. When the time arrived for the crowning of the victor, the candidate was brought forward in presence of a vast concourse of spectators, and placed upon a tripod, which was originally formed of bronze, but in subsequent ages was wrought in ivory and gold. Branches of palm-trees, the usual symbols of victory, were placed in his hands. His name and that of his father and of the country whence he came, were proclaimed with great ceremony by the heralds. The crown was then placed upon his head, and the festival ended with processions and sacrifices and a public banquet given in honor of the occasion. On his return to his own country, the victor entered the capital by a triumphal procession, and was usually rewarded there by immunities and privileges of the most important character.

At length the time arrived for the celebration of the Olympic games, and Nero repaired to the spot, following the vast throngs that were proceeding thither from every part of Greece, and there entered into competition with all the common singers and players of the time. The prize for excellence in music was awarded to him. It was, however, generally understood that the judges were bribed to decide in his favor. Nero entered as a competitor, too, in the chariot race; and here he was successful in winning the prize; though in this case it was decreed to him in plain and open violation of all rule. He undertook to drive ten horses in this race; but he found the team too much for him to control. The horses became unmanageable; Nero was thrown out of his carriage and was so much hurt that he could not finish the race at all. He, however, insisted that accidents and casualties were not to be taken into the account, and that inasmuch as he should certainly have outran his competitors if he had not been prevented by misfortune, he claimed that the judges should award him the prize. Greatly to his delight the judges did so. It is true they were bound by the most solemn oaths to make just and true decisions; but it has been seldom found in the history of the world that official oaths constitute any serious barrier against the demands or encroachments of emperors or kings.

When the games were ended Nero conferred very rich rewards upon all the judges.

These successes at the Olympic games, nominal and empty as they really were, seemed to have inflamed the emperor's vanity and ambition more than ever. Instead of returning to Rome he commenced another tour through the heart of Greece, singing and playing in all the cities where he went, and challenging all the most distinguished actors and performers to meet him and contend with him for prizes.

Of course the prizes were always awarded to Nero on this tour, as they had been at the Olympic games. Nero sent home regular dispatches after each of his performances, to inform the Roman Senate of his victories, just as former emperors had been accustomed to send military bulletins to announce the progress of their armies, and the conquests which they had gained in battle; and with a degree of vanity and folly which seems almost incredible, he called upon the Senate to institute religious celebrations and sacrifices in Rome, and great public processions, in order to signalize and commemorate these great successes, and to express the gratitude of the people to the gods for having vouchsafed them. Not satisfied with expecting this parade of public rejoicing in Rome, he called upon the Senate to ordain that similar services should be held in all the cities and towns throughout the empire.

During the visit of Nero to Greece, he engaged in one undertaking which might be denominated a useful enterprise, though he managed it with such characteristic imbecil-

ity and folly, that it ended, as might have
been foreseen, in a miserable failure. The
plan which he conceived, was to cut through
the Isthmus of Corinth, so as to open a ship
communication between the Ionian and the
Ægean seas. Such a canal, he thought,
would save for many vessels the long and
dangerous voyage around the Peloponnesus,
and thus prevent many of the wrecks which
then annually took place on the shores of the
Peninsula, and which were often attended
with the destruction of much property and of
many lives.

The plan might thus have been a very good
one, had any proper and efficient means been
adopted for carrying it into execution; but
in all that he did in this respect, Nero seems
to have looked no farther than to the performance of pompous and empty ceremonies in
commencing the work. He convened a great
public assembly on the ground. He entertained this assembly with spectacles and
shows. He then placed himself at the head
of his life-guards, and, after a speech of great
promise and pretension, he advanced at the
head of a procession, singing and dancing by
the way, to the place where the first ground

was to be broken. Here he made three
strokes with a golden pick-axe, which had
been provided for the occasion, and putting
the earth which he had loosened into a
basket, he carried it away to a short distance,
and threw it out upon the ground. This
ceremony was meant for the commencement
of the canal; and when it was over, the
company dispersed, and Nero was escorted
by his guards back to the city of Corinth,
which lay at a few miles' distance from the
scene.

Nothing more was ever done. Nero issued
orders, it is true, that all the criminals, convicts, and prisoners in Greece, should be
transported to the Isthmus, and set to work
upon this canal; and some Jewish captives
were actually employed there for a time;
but, for some reason or other, nothing was
done. The actual work was never seriously
undertaken.

In the mean time, Nero had left the government at Rome in the hands of a certain
ignoble favorite, named Helius, who, being
placed in command of the army during his
master's absence, held the lives and fortunes
of all the inhabitants at his supreme disposal,

15—19

and, as might have been expected, he pursued such a career of cruelty and oppression,
in his attempts to overawe and subject those
who were under his power, that a universal
feeling of hostility and hatred was awakened
against him. Things at last assumed so
alarming an attitude, that Helius was terrified in his turn, and at length he began to
send for Nero to come home. Nero at first
paid no attention to these requests. The
danger, however, increased; the crisis became extremely imminent, so that a general
insurrection was anticipated. Helius sent
messengers after messengers to Nero, imploring him to return, if he wished to save himself from ruin;—but all the answer that he
could obtain from Nero was, that, if Helius
truly loved him, he would not envy him the
glory that he was acquiring in Greece; but,
instead of hastening his return, would rather
wish that he should come back worthy of
himself, after having fully accomplished his
victories. At last Helius, growing desperate
in view of the impending danger, left Rome,
and, traveling with all possible dispatch,
night and day, came to Nero in Greece, and
there made such statements and disclosures

in respect to the condition of things at Rome,
that Nero at length reluctantly concluded to
return.

He accordingly set out in grand state on
his journey westward, escorted by his body-
guard, and with his motley and innumerable
horde of singers, dancers, poets, actors, and
mountebanks in his train. He brought with
him the prizes which he had won in the various cities of Greece. The number of these
prizes, it was said, was more than eighteen
hundred. On his way through Greece, when
about to return to Rome, he went to Delphi,
to consult the sacred oracle there, in respect
to his future fortunes. The reply of the
Pythoness was, "*Beware of seventy-three.*"
This answer gave Nero great satisfaction and
pleasure. It meant, he had no doubt, that
he had no danger to fear until he should have
attained to the age of seventy-three; and as
he was yet not quite thirty, the response of
the oracle seemed to put so far away the evil
day, that he thought he might dismiss it from
his mind altogether. So he repaid the oracle
for the flattering prediction with most magnificent presents, and pursued his journey toward Rome with a mind quite at ease

292   N E R O.   [A.D. 66

His voyage.   Danger of shipwreck.   Journey to Rome

The ships in which he embarked to cross the Adriatic on his return to Italy encountered a terrible storm, by which they were dispersed, and many of them were destroyed Nero himself had a very narrow escape, as the ship which he was in came very near being lost. To see him in this danger seems greatly to have pleased some of his attendants, for so imperious and cruel was his temper, that he was generally hated by all who came under his power. These men hated him so intensely that they were willing, as it would appear, to perish themselves, for the pleasure of witnessing his destruction; and in the extreme moments of danger they openly manifested this feeling. The vessel, however, was saved, and Nero, as soon as he landed, ordered these persons all to be slain.

On landing he gathered together the scattered remnants of his company, and organizing a new escort, he advanced toward Rome, in a grand triumphal march, displaying his prizes and crowns in all the great cities through which he passed, and claiming universal homage. When he arrived at the gates of Rome, he made preparations for a grand triumphal entry to the city, in the man ner of great military conquerors. A breach was made in the walls for the admission of the procession. Nero rode in the triumpnal chariot of Augustus, with a distinguished Greek harpist by his side, who wore an Olympic crown upon his head, and carried another crown in his hand. Before this chariot marched a company of eighteen hundred men, each of them carrying one of the crowns which Nero had won, with an inscription for the spectators to read, signifying where the crown had been won, the name of the emperor's competitor, the title of the song which he had sung, and other similar particulars. In this way he traversed the principal streets, exhibiting himself and his trophies to the populace, and finally when he arrived at his house, he entered it with great pomp and parade, and caused the crowns to be hung up upon the innumerable statues of himself which had been erected in the courts and halls of the building. Those which he valued most highly he placed conspicuously around his bed in his bedchamber, in order that they might be the last objects for his eyes to rest upon at night, and the first to greet his view in the morning.

19

As soon as he became established in Rome again, he began to form new plans for developing his powers and capacities as a musician, in the hope of gaining still higher triumphs than those to which he had already attained. Far from giving his time and attention to the public business of the empire, he devoted himself with new zeal and enthusiasm to the cultivation of his art. In doing this it was necessary, according to the customs and usages in respect to the training of musicians that prevailed in those days, that he should submit to rules and exercises most absurd and degrading to one holding such a station as his ; and as accounts of his mode of life circulated among the community, he became an object of general ridicule and contempt. In order to strengthen his lungs and improve his voice he used to lie on his back with a plate of lead upon his chest, that the lungs, working under such a burden, might acquire strength by the effort. He took powerful medicines, such as were supposed in those days to act upon the system in such a manner as to produce clearness and resonance in the tones of the voice. He subjected himself to the most rigid rules of diet,—and gave up the practice of addressing the senate and the army, which the Roman emperors often had occasion to do, for fear that speaking so loud might strain his voice and injure the sweetness of its tones. He had a special officer in his household, called his *Phonascus*, meaning his voice-keeper. This officer was to watch him at all times, caution him against speaking too loud or too fast,—prescribe for him, and in every way take care that his voice received no detriment. During all this time Nero was continually performing in public, and though his performances were protracted and tedious to the last degree, all the Roman nobility were compelled always to attend them, under pain of his horrible displeasure.

As Nero went on thus in the career which he had chosen,—neglecting altogether the affairs of government, and giving himself up more and more every year to the most expensive dissipation; his finances became at length greatly involved, and he was compelled to resort to every possible form of extortion, in order to raise the money that he required. His pecuniary embarrassments became, at length, very perplexing, and they were finally very much increased by the extraordinary folly which he displayed in giving credence to the dreams and promises of a certain adventurer who came to him from Africa. The name of this man was Bessus. He was a native of Carthage. He came, at one time, to Rome, and having contrived, by means of presents and bribes which he offered to the officers of Nero's household, to obtain an audience of the emperor, he informed him that he had intelligence of the highest importance to communicate, which was, that on his estate in Africa, there was a large cavern, in which was stored an immense treasure. This treasure consisted, he said, of vast heaps of golden ingots, rude and shapeless in form, but composed of pure and precious metal. The cavern, he said, which contained these stores, was very spacious, and the gold lay piled in it in heaps, and sometimes in solid columns, towering to a prodigious height. These treasures had been deposited there, he said, by Dido, the ancient Carthaginian queen, and they had remained there so long, that all knowledge of them had been lost. They had been reserved, in a word, for Nero, and were all now at his disposal, ready to be brought out and employed in promoting the glory and magnificence of his reign.

Nero readily gave credit to this story, an inasmuch as in the exuberance of his exultation he made known this wonderful discovery to those around him, the tidings of it soon spread throughout the city, and produced the most intense excitement among all classes. Nero immediately began to fit out an expedition to proceed to Africa, and bring the treasure home. Galleys were equipped to convey it, and a body of troops was designated to escort it, and suitable officers appointed to proceed with Bessus to Carthage, and superintend the transportation of the metal. These preparations necessarily required some time, and during the interval Bessus was of course the object at Rome of universal attention and regard. Nero himself, finding that he was about to enter upon the possession of such inexhaustible treasures, dismissed all concern in respect to his finances, and launched out into wilder extravagance than ever. He raised money for the present moment, by assigning shares in the treasure at exorbitant rates of

discount, and thus borrowed and expended
with the most unbounded profusion.

At length the expedition sailed for Carthage, taking Bessus with them,—but all
search for the cavern, when they arrived, was
unavailing. It proved that all the evidence
which Bessus had of the existence of the cave,
and of the heaps of gold contained in it, was
derived from certain remarkable dreams which
he had had,—and though Nero's commissioners dug into the ground most faithfully in
every place on the estate which the dreams
had indicated, no treasure, and not even the
cavern, could ever be found.

Chapter XIII.

Nero's End.

THE successor of Nero in the line of Roman emperors, was Galba. Galba, though a son of one of the most illustrious Roman families, was born in Spain, and he was about forty years older than Nero, being now over seventy, while Nero was yet but thirty years of age.

During the whole course of his life, Galba had been a very distinguished commander, and had risen from one post of influence and honor to another, until he became one of the most considerable personages in the state. Nero at length appointed him to the command of a very large and important province in Spain. At this station Galba remained some years, and he was here, attending regularly to the duties of his government, at the time when Nero returned from his expedition into Greece. Galba himself, and all the other governors around him, felt the same indignation at Nero's cruelties and crimes, and the

same contempt for his low and degrading
vanity and folly, that prevailed so generally
at Rome. In fact, feelings of exasperation
and hatred against the tyrant, began to ex-
tend universally throughout the empire. The
people in every quarter, in fact, seemed ripe
for insurrection.

While things were in this state, a messenger arrived one day at Galba's court, from a
certain chieftain of the Gauls, named Julius
Vindex. This messenger came to announce
to Galba that Vindex had revolted against the
Roman government in Gaul. He declared,
however, that it was only *Nero's* power that
Vindex intended to resist, and promised that
if Galba would himself assume the supreme
command, Vindex would acknowledge allegiance to him, and would do all in his power
to promote his cause. He said, moreover,
that such was the detestation in which Nero
was universally held, that there was no doubt
that the whole empire would sustain Galba in
effecting such a revolution, if he would once
raise his standard. At the same time that
this messenger came from Vindex, another
came from the Roman governor of the province of Gaul, where Vindex resided, to inform

Galba of the revolt, and asking for a detachment of troops to assist him in putting it down. Galba called a council, and laid the subject before them.

After some debate one of the councillors rose and said that there was no more danger in openly joining Vindex in his rebellion, than here was in debating, in such a council, what they should do. "It is just as treasonable," said he, "to doubt and hesitate whether to send troops to put down the revolt, as it would be openly to rebel; and Nero will so regard it. My counsel therefore is that, unless you choose to be considered as aiding the revolution, you should instantly send off troops to put it down."

Galba was much impressed with the wisdom of this advice. He felt strongly inclined to favor the cause of Vindex and the rebels, and on further reflection he secretly determined to join them, and to take measures for raising a general insurrection. He did not, however, make known his determination to any one, but dismissed the council without declaring what he had concluded to do. Soon afterward he sent out to all parts of the province, and ordered a general mustering of the

forces under his command, and of all that
could be raised throughout the province, requiring them to meet at a certain appointed
rendezvous.   The army, though not openly
informed of it, suspected what the object of
this movement was to be, and came forward
to the work, with the utmost alacrity and joy.

In the mean time the tidings of Vindex's
revolt traveled rapidly to Rome, and thence
to Naples, where Nero was at this time performing on the public stage.   Nero seemed to
be very much delighted to hear the news.
He supposed that the rebellion would of
course be very easily suppressed, and that
when it was suppressed he could make it an
excuse for subjecting the province in which it
had occurred to fines and confiscations that
would greatly enrich his treasury.   He was
extremely pleased therefore at the tidings of
the revolt, and abandoned himself to the theatrical pursuits and pleasures in which he was
engaged, more absolutely and recklessly than
ever.

In the mean time fresh messengers arrived
at short intervals from Rome, to inform Nero
of the progress of the rebellion.   The news
was that Vindex was gaining strength every

day, and was issuing proclamations to the
people calling upon them everywhere to rise
and throw off the ignoble yoke of oppression
which they were enduring. In these proclamations the emperor was called Brazenbeard,
and designated as a "wretched fiddler."
These taunts excited Nero's ire. He wrote to
the Senate at Rome calling upon them to
adopt some measures for putting down this
insolent rebel, and having dispatched this
letter, he seemed to dismiss the subject from
his mind, and turned his attention anew to
his dancing and acting.

His mind was, however, soon disturbed
again, for fresh messengers continued to come,
each bringing reports more alarming than
those of his predecessor. The rebellion was
evidently gaining ground. Nero was convinced that something must be done. He accordingly broke away, though with great reluctance, from his amusements at Naples, and
proceeded to Rome. On his arrival at the
capital he called a council of some of his principal ministers of state, and after a short consultation on the subject of the rebellion—in
which, however, nothing was determined
upon—he proceeded to produce some newly-

invented musical instruments which he had
brought with him from Naples, and in which
he was greatly interested. After showing
and explaining these instruments to the councilors, he promised them that he would give
them the pleasure before long of hearing a
performance upon them, on the stage,—
"provided," he added jocosely, "that this
Vindex will give me leave."

The councilors at length withdrew, and
Nero remained in his apartment. On retiring
to rest, however, he found that he could not
sleep. His thoughts were running on the
musical instruments which he had been showing, and on the pleasure which he anticipated
in a public performance with them. At
length, at a very late hour, he sent for his
councilors to come again to his apartment.
They came, full of excitement and wonder,
supposing that they were thus suddenly summoned on account of some new and very
momentous tidings which had been received
from Gaul. They found, however, that Nero
only wished to give some farther account of
the instruments which he had shown them,
and to ask their opinions of certain improve-

ments which had occurred to him since they went away.

Nero did not, however, remain very long in this state of insane and stupid unconcern; for on the evening of the following day a courier arrived from the north with the appalling intelligence that Vindex had made himself master of Gaul, and that Galba, the most powerful general in the Roman army, had joined the insurrection with all the legions under his command, and that he was now advancing toward Rome at the head of his armies with the avowed purpose of deposing Nero, and making himself emperor in his stead.

Nero was at first absolutely stupefied at hearing these tidings. He remained for some time silent and motionless, as if made completely senseless with consternation. When at length he came to himself again, he fell into a perfect frenzy of rage and terror. He overturned the supper table, tore his garments, threw down two valuable cups to the floor and broke them to pieces, and then began to dash his head against the wall, as if he were perfectly insane. He said he was undone. No man had ever been so wretched. His domin-

15—20

ions were to be seized from him while he yet lived, and held by an usurper; he was utterly ruined and undone.

After a little time had elapsed the agitation and excitement of his mind took another direction, that of furious anger against the generals and officers of his army,—not only those who had actually rebelled, but all others, for he was jealous and suspicious of all, and said that he believed that the whole army was engaged in the conspiracy. He was going to send out orders to the various provinces and encampments, for the assassination of great numbers of the officers,—such as he imagined might be inclined to turn against him,—and he would probably have done so if he had not been restrained by the influence of his ministers of state. He also proposed to seize and kill all the Gauls then in Rome, as a mode of taking vengeance on their countrymen for joining Vindex in his rebellion, and could scarcely be prevented from doing this by the urgent remonstrances of all his friends.

After a time Nero so far recovered his self possession that he began to make preparations for organizing an army, with the design of marching against the rebels. He accordingly

ordered troops to be enlisted and arms and
ammunition to be provided,—assessing at the
same time heavy taxes upon the people of
Rome to defray the expense. All these
arrangements, however, only increased the
general discontent. The people saw that the
preparations which the emperor was making
were wholly inadequate to the crisis, and that
no efficient military operations could ever
come from them. In the first place, he could
obtain no troops, for no men fit for soldiers
were willing to enlist,—and so he undertook
to supply the deficiency by requiring every
master of slaves to send him a certain number
of his bondmen, and these bondmen he freed
and then enrolled them in his army, in lieu
of soldiers. Moreover, in making provision
for the wants of his army, instead of devoting
his chief attention to securing a sufficiency of
arms, ammunition, military stores, and other
such supplies as were required in preparing
for an efficient campaign, he seemed only interested in getting together actors, dancers,
musical instruments, and dresses for performers on the public stage. In excuse for this
course of procedure, Nero said frankly that
ne did not expect that his expedition would

lead to any important military operations. As soon as he reached the rebel armies his intention was, he said, to throw himself upon their sense of justice and their loyalty. He would acknowledge whatever had been wrong in his past government, and promise solemnly that his sway in future should be more mild and beneficent; and he had no doubt that thus the whole disturbance would be quelled. The revolted troops would at once return to their duty, and the musical and theatrical preparations which he was making were intended for a series of grand festivities to celebrate the reconciliation.

Of course such insane and hopeless folly as this awakened a sentiment of universal contempt and indignation among the people of Rome. The greatest excitement and confusion prevailed throughout the city; and, as is usual in times of public panic, money and provisions were hid away by those who possessed them, in secret hoards; and this soon occasioned a great scarcity of food. The city, in fact, was threatened with famine. In the midst of the alarm and anxiety which this state of things occasioned, two ships arrived from Egypt, at Ostia, and the news produced a general rejoicing,—it being supposed, of course, that the ships were laden with corn. It proved, however, that there was no corn on board. Instead of food for the metropolis, the cargo consisted of *sand*, intended to form the *arena* of some of the emperor's amphitheaters, for the gladiators and wrestlers to stand upon, in contending. This incident seemed to fill the cup of public indignation to the brim; and, as news arrived just at this time that the rebellion had extended into Germany, and that all the legions in the German provinces had gone over to Galba, Nero's power began to be considered at an end. Tumults prevailed everywhere throughout the city, and assemblies were held, threatening open defiance to the authority of the emperor, and declaring the readiness of the people to acknowledge Galba so soon as he should arrive.

Nero was now more terrified than ever. He knew not what to do. He fled from his palace, and sought a retreat in certain gardens near—acting in this, however, under the influence of a blind and instinctive fear, rather than from any rational hope of securing his safety by seeking such a place of refuge.

20

In fact, he was now perfectly distracted with
terror. He procured some poison before he
left his palace, and carried it in a small golden
box with him to the gardens; but he had not
strength or resolution to take it. He then
conceived of the plan of flying from Rome
altogether. He would go at once to Ostia,
he said, and there embark on board a ship
and sail for Egypt, where, it might be supposed, he would be out of the reach of his
enemies. He asked his officers and attendants if they would accompany him in this
flight. But they refused to go.

Then he began to talk of another plan. He
would go and meet Galba as a suppliant, and,
falling upon his knees before the conqueror,
would implore him to spare his life. Or he
would go into the Roman Forum, and make
a humble and supplicatory address to the
people there, imploring their forgiveness for
his cruelties and crimes, and solemnly prom-
ising never to be guilty of such excesses
again, if they would pardon and protect him.
The by-standers told him that such a proceeding was wholly out of the question; for if he
were to go forth for such a purpose from his
retreat, the people were in such a frenzy of

excitement against him, that they would tear
him to pieces before he could reach the Ros-
tra. In a word, the distracted thoughts of
the wretched criminal turned this way and
that, in the wild agitation with which remorse and terror filled his mind, vainly seeking some way of escape from the awful
dangers which were circling and narrowing
so rapidly around him. There was, in fact,
no hope now left for him—no refuge, no
protection, no possibility of escape; and so,
after suddenly seizing, and as suddenly abandoning, one impracticable scheme after another, his mind became wholly bewildered,
and he sank down, at length, into a condition
of blank and hopeless despair.

Although the insurrection had become very
general in the provinces, the troops in the
city, consisting chiefly of the emperor's
guards, yet remained faithful; and now as
the night was coming on, they were stationed
as usual at their respective posts in various
parts of the city and at the palace gates.
Nero retired to rest. He found, however, that
ne could not sleep. At midnight he rose,
and came forth from his apartment. He was
surprised to find that there was no sentinel at

312   NERO.   [A.D. 67.

He is deserted by his guards.   He calls for a gladiator.

the door. On farther examination he found
to his amazement that the palace guards had
been wholly withdrawn. He was thunderstruck at making this discovery. He returned into the palace and aroused some of
the domestics, and then went forth with them
to the residences of some of his chief ministers, who resided near, to ask for help. He
could, however, nowhere gain admission. He
found the houses all closely shut up, and by
all his knocking at the doors he could get no
answer from any persons within. He then
came back in great distress and alarm to his
own apartment. He found that it had been
broken into during the short time that he had
been gone, and rifled of every thing valuable
that it contained. Even his golden box of
poison had been carried away. In a word the
great sovereign of half the world found that
he had been abandoned by all his adherents,
and left in a condition of utter and absolute
exposure. The guards had concluded to de-
clare for Galba, and had accordingly gone
away, leaving the fallen tyrant to his fate.

Nero called desperately to his servants to
send for a gladiator to thrust him through
with a sword, but no one would go. "Alas!"

ne exclaimed, "has it come to this?   Am I
so utterly abandoned that I have not even
enemies left who are willing to kill me?"

After a little time he began to be a little
more composed, and expressed a wish that he
knew of some place in the environs of the city
where he could go and conceal himself for a
little time until he could determine what to
do.   One of the servants of his household
named Phaon, told him that he had a country-
house near the city, where, perhaps, Nero
might hide.   Nero immediately resolved to
go there.   The better to conceal his flight he
disguised himself in mean apparel, and tied
a handkerchief about his face; and then
mounting on horseback in company with two
or three attendants, he proceeded out of the
city.   As he went, it thundered and lightened
from time to time, and Nero was greatly ter
rified.   He supposed that the commotion of
the elements was occasioned by the spirits of
those whom he had murdered coming now to
persecute and torment him in the hour of his
extremity.

He passed, during his ride, a station of the
guard which happened to be on his way, and
heard the soldiers cursing him as he went by.

and expressing joy at his downfall. Soon after
this he overheard a passenger whom his party
met on the road, say to his companion, when
he saw Nero and his attendants riding by,
"These men no doubt are going in pursuit of
the emperor." Another man whom they met
on the way stopped them to ask what news
there was in town about the emperor. In
these occurrences, though they of course
tended to increase the agitation and excitement of Nero's mind, there was nothing particularly alarming; but at length an incident
happened which frightened the fugitive extremely. He was passing a place where a
carcass lay by the side of the road. Some
soldiers of the guard were standing near.
The horse that Nero rode was startled at the
sight of the carcass, and springing suddenly
shook down the handkerchief from Nero's
face. One of the soldiers by this means obtained a view of his countenance, and exclaimed that that was the emperor. Nero
was so much alarmed at this that he hastened
on, and as soon as he was out of the view of
the men who had seen him, he leaped from
his horse, and calling upon his attendants to
dismount too and follow him, he ran into

He refuses to be buried before he is dead.

an adjoining thicket, among bushes and briers, and thence the whole party made their
way circuitously round to the rear of Phaon's
grounds. Here they stopped and hid themselves till they could contrive some way to
get through or over the wall.

There was a pit near by, which had been
made by digging for sand. Phaon proposed
that Nero should hide in this pit until an
opening could be made in the wall. But
Nero refused to do this, saying that he would
not be buried before he was dead. So he remained hid in the thickets while Phaon went
to work to make an opening in the wall.

The wall was not of a very substantial
character; if it had been, it would not have
been possible for Phaon, with the means at
his command, to have effected a passage.
As it was, he succeeded, though with difficulty, in loosening some of the stones, so as
gradually to make an opening.

Nero was engaged, while this work was going
on, in pulling the briers out of his clothes and
flesh, and being thirsty, he went down to a
ditch that was near, and drank, taking up
the water in his hands. As he drank, he

316　　　　　Nero.　　　　[A.D. 67.

He gets through the wall.　　　　　He is concealed.

PHAON AT THE WALL.

groaned out, "Oh, can it be that I have come to this!"

In the mean time, Phaon went on with his work, and soon succeeded in making a hole in the wall sufficient for his purpose, and then the men dragged Nero through. They brought him into the house, and shut him up in a small and secret apartment there.

Nero now felt relieved from the extreme terror which he had suffered during his flight;

but the feelings of terror subsided in his mind, only to give place to the still more dreadful pangs of remorse and horror. He moaned continually in his anguish, and incessantly repeated the words, "My father, my mother, and my wife doom me to destruction." These were indeed the words of one of the tragedies which he had been accustomed to act upon the stage, but they expressed the remorse and anguish of his mind so truly, that they recurred continually to his lips. Phaon and the men who had brought him to the house, finding it impossible to calm him, and seeing no hope of his final escape from death, and perhaps, moreover, wishing to relieve themselves of what was now fast becoming a serious burthen to them, recommended to him to kill himself,—and thus, as they said, since he must die, die like a man. Finally, Nero seemed to yield to their urgings. He said that he would kill himself as they desired They might go out and dig a grave for him, and prepare wood and water for washing the body. While giving these orders he moaned and groaned continually, as if in a state of delirium.

In the mean time the morning had come,

and at Rome all was excitement and commotion. The Senate came together and proclaimed Galba. emperor. They also passed a decree pronouncing Nero an enemy to the state, and sentencing him to be punished as such in the ancient manner. When this news transpired, a friend of Phaon wrote a letter to him, giving an account of what the Senate had done, and sent it off with the utmost haste by a trusty messenger. The messenger arrived at Phaon's house, and brought the letter in. Nero seized it from Phaon's hands, and read it. "What is the ancient manner?" he asked, in a tone of great anxiety and terror. They told him that it was to be stripped naked, and then to be secured by having his head fastened in a pillory, and in that position to be whipped to death. At hearing this, Nero broke forth in fresh groans and lamentations. He could not endure such a death as that, he said, and he would kill himself, therefore, at once, if they would give him a dagger.

There were daggers at hand. Nero took them, examined the points of them with a trembling touch, seemed undecided, and finally put them away again, saying that his hour was not yet quite come. Presently he

took one of the daggers again, and made a
new attempt to awaken in himself sufficient
resolution to strike the blow, but his courage
failed him. He moaned and raved all this
time in the most incoherent and distracted
manner. He even begged that one of the
attendants who were with him would take the
dagger and kill himself first, in order to encourage Nero by letting him see that it was
not after all so dreadful a thing to die. But
no one of the attendants seemed sufficiently
devoted to his master to be willing to render
him such a service as this.

In the midst of this perplexity and delay a
noise was heard as of horsemen riding up to
the door. Nero was terrified anew at the
sound. They were coming, he said, to seize
him. He immediately drew one of the daggers, and putting it to his throat, attempted desperately to nerve himself to the work
of driving it home. But he could not do it.
The noise at the door in the mean time increased. Nero then gave the dagger to one
of the men standing by, and begged that he
would kill him. The man took the dagger
with great reluctance, but presently gave the

320   NERO.   [A.D. 67

The soldiers attempt to save Nero.   He dies.

fatal stab, and Nero sank down upon the ground mortally wounded.

At this moment the door was suddenly opened, and the soldiers that had just arrived came in. They had been sent by the Senate to search for the fugitive and bring him back to Rome. The centurion who commanded these men, advanced into the room, and looked at the fallen emperor, as he lay upon the floor, weltering in his blood. He had been commanded to bring the prisoner to the city, if possible, alive; and he accordingly ordered the soldiers to come to the dying man and endeavor to stanch his wounds and save him. But it was too late. Nero stared at them as they advanced to take hold of him, with a wild and frightful expression of countenance, which shocked all who saw him, and in the midst of this agony of terror, he sank down and died.

The news of the tyrant's death spread with the utmost rapidity in all directions. A courier immediately set off for the north to carry tidings of the event to Galba. People flocked from all quarters to the house of Pnaon to gaze on the lifeless body, and to exult in the monster's death. The people of the city gave themselves up to the wildest and most extravagant joy. They put on caps such as were worn by manumitted slaves when first obtaining their freedom, and roamed about the city expressing in every possible way the exultation they felt at their deliverance, and breaking down and destroying the statues of Nero wherever they could find them.

In the mean time Galba was steadily advancing on the way to Rome. In due time he made his entry into the city, and embassadors came to him there from all parts of the Roman world to acknowledge him as the reigning emperor. At this time he was seventy-three years old. So that the number seventy-three of which the oracle had warned Nero to beware, denoted the age of his rival and enemy,—not his own.

15—21

THE END.